MIES VAN DER ROHE: ARCHITECT AS EDUCATOR

6 June through 12 July 1986

Catalogue for the exhibition
edited by Rolf Achilles, Kevin Harrington,
and Charlotte Myhrum

Mies van der Rohe Centennial Project
Illinois Institute of Technology, Chicago

The Mies van der Rohe Centennial Project dedicates this catalogue to John Augur Holabird, Sr., FAIA, (May 4, 1886–May 4, 1945), respected friend of Ludwig Mies van der Rohe.
His initiative and vision as Trustee of Armour Institute of Technology and as Chairman of its Search Committee which brought Mies to Chicago contributed significantly to changing the course of architectural education in America.

Funding of the Centennial Project and exhibition has been provided by the Graham Foundation for Advanced Studies in the Fine Arts, the National Endowment for the Humanities, the Illinois Arts Council, a state agency, the New House Foundation, the S.O.M. Foundation and the following individuals: Michael E. Breen, Peter Carter, Molly Cohen, George Danforth, Joseph Fujikawa, Myron Goldsmith, Warren Haber, John Holabird, Jr., Phyllis Lambert, Dirk Lohan, John Neil, Peter Palumbo, H.P. Davis Rockwell, John B. Rodgers, Gene Summers and Steven Weiss.

Cover photo: Experimental photograph. Photographer unknown. Collection of Edward A. Duckett. Catalogue number 135.

Frontispiece: Mies van der Rohe with model of S. R. Crown Hall. Photograph by Arthur Siegel. Courtesy Chicago Historical Society.

The catalogue is distributed by The University of Chicago Press

Library of Congress Catalogue Card Number 86-71034
Clothbound: ISBN 0-226-31716-1; Paperbound: ISBN 0-226-31718-8.

Designed by Harvey Retzloff
Composition by Computype™
Printed in the United States of America
by Congress Printing Company

CONTENTS

LENDERS TO THE EXHIBITION

The Art Institute of Chicago

Bauhaus Archiv, Berlin

Berliner Bild-Bericht, Berlin

Thomas Burleigh

Canadian Centre for Architecture, Montreal

Chicago Historical Society

George Danforth

Edward A. Duckett

Mark Finfer

Kenneth Folgers

Joseph Fujikawa

Feico Glastra van Loon

Albert Goers

Myron Goldsmith

Ogden Hannaford

R. Lawrence J. Harrison

Hedrich Blessing

John Burgee Architects with Philip Johnson

Raymond Kliphardt

Reginald Malcolmson

Carter H. Manny, Jr.

Marcia Gray Martin

John Munson

Brigitte Peterhans

Richard Nickel Committee

Norman Ross

Rudolf Kicken Galerie, Cologne

David Sharpe

Malcolm Smith

Edward Starostovic

George Storz

David Tamminga

Michael Van Beuren

John Vinci

Yau Chun Wong

Donald Wrobleski

Edmond N. Zisook

ACKNOWLEDGMENTS

Several years ago, when the centennial of Mies's birth seemed far away, some people in Chicago and New York began to think about the event and how best to honor the memory of a great architect and teacher. It was soon agreed that the two important repositories of Mies's legacy, the Department of Architecture, Illinois Institute of Technology, Chicago and the Mies Archive, the Museum of Modern Art, New York, should mount independent exhibitions — one concentrating on its legacy, the other on its holdings. In this way IIT developed its exhibition and catalogue — *Mies van der Rohe: Architect as Educator* and MoMA organized its *Mies van der Rohe Centennial Exhibition*. By showing both exhibitions together in Chicago and in Berlin, the two centers of Mies's life, his impact on the 20th Century could be thoroughly explored. Both exhibits, each in its own way, emphasize a unique aspect of the man, Ludwig Mies van der Rohe, educator and architect.

Many people have worked to create the IIT exhibit and catalogue. None has contributed more than George Danforth, Mies's student, colleague, and successor as Director of the School of Architecture. George's seemingly personal acquaintance with every student who attended IIT from 1938 to 1958 and his continued interest in their careers is the foundation upon which this exhibit and its catalogue is built. George's selfless interest in creating the finest possible tribute to Mies as educator has been an inspiration to those fortunate enough to be his colleagues. Without his memory, initiative, attention to detail, humor, typing skills, sure eye, bullying at just the right moment those that need it, and ever-present good humor, much of what follows in this publication would not be.

Others have also helped to create this catalogue and the exhibition. In January 1983 Thomas L. Martin, Jr., President of IIT, established the Centennial Advisory Committee, co-chaired by George Danforth and John Holabird, Jr., architect and son of the chairman of the committee that brought Mies to Chicago. Other Committee members were Peter Beltemacchi, Harold Bergen, Heather Bilandic, Myron Goldsmith, Archibald McClure, Nancy Moss, George Schipporeit, David Sharpe, Arthur Takeuchi, James Vice, Willard White, representing trustees, administrators and faculty. George Schipporeit, Dean of the College of Architecture, Planning, and Design has acted as Project Director. Carter H. Manny, Jr. served as chairman of the Committee of Friends. Arthur Takeuchi organized the series of eight lectures sponsored by IIT with assistance from The Art Institute of Chicago and the Goethe Institute Chicago. The executive body for the Mies Centennial Project, the Planning Committee, originally consisted of George Danforth, Myron Goldsmith, George Schipporeit, David Sharpe, Arthur Takeuchi, and T. Paul Young. Initially the Project Curator, T. Paul Young with the assistance of Billie McGrew, Project Assistant, prepared a broad range of planning documents, reports, and the N.E.H. grant application on which the Project is based. The foundation they laid enabled the Project to achieve its purpose.

In the fall of 1984 and again in the spring of 1985, John Sugden, David Haid and Arthur Takeuchi organized two weekend long colloquia at the Graham Foundation for students, former colleagues and friends of Mies. These two events proved to be very important catalysts for the Project. They gave it direction and meaning, and further helped all those who attended to better understand the state of knowledge and interest in the work and life of Mies.

Special thanks to Phyllis Lambert for her keen interest in the exhibition's direction and guidance in selecting essayists for the catalogue; and Dirk Lohan for his suggestions and support.

The day-to-day direction of the Project has been accomplished by Rolf Achilles, with the assistance of George Danforth and Charlotte Myhrum. John Vinci curated and designed the exhibition with the assistance of George Danforth and Charlotte Myhrum.

A number of students contributed to the Project. Outstanding among these is Donna J. Junkroski who through dozens of hours of reviewing microfilm and old class records created a complete list of students, faculty and their classes during Mies's tenure as Director. Other students who assisted the Project were George Sorich, model builder, Laurie Grimmer and Michael Patton.

In the College of Architecture, Planning, and Design, help was forthcoming from San Utsunomiya and Bernie Ivers, Assistant Deans, Catherine Howard and Sylvia Smith in the College Office and the Dean of the College, George Schipporeit.

In the professional community many colleagues have been very cooperative. We are especially indebted to the Bauhaus Archiv, Berlin and its Director Dr. Peter Hahn for his very generous assistance to the point of co-sponsorship of this exhibit in Berlin. We are also deeply in debt for his subvention of photographic expenses and the German language edition of this catalogue. His colleague at the Bauhaus Archiv, Dr. Christian Wolsdorff has been instrumental in securing photographs of the loaned works and assuring proper shipment of the works to Chicago. Arthur Drexler, Director of the Department of Architecture and Design at the Museum of Modern Art, New York, has been most helpful, as have Eve Blau of the Canadian Centre for Architecture, Montreal, and Suzanne Pastor of the Kicken Galerie, Cologne. Malcolm Richardson, Program Officer in the Division of General Programs at the National Endowment for the Humanities, provided guidance and encouragement when the fate of the Project looked most bleak.

In Chicago we especially thank John Zukowsky, Curator of the Department of Architecture at The Art Institute of Chicago, Nell McClure, Director of the Chicago Architecture Foundation and its Education Director, Paul Glassman for coordinating tours; Wim de Wit, Curator of the Architectural Collection at the Chicago Historical Society; Dr. Walter Breuer, Director, and Angela Greiner, Program Assistant at the Goethe Institute Chicago; Carter H. Manny, Jr., Director of the Graham Foundation for Advanced Studies in the Fine Arts; the staff of *Inland Architect*; Franz Schulze; I. Michael Danoff, Director of the Museum of Contemporary Art and its Director of Public Relations, Lisa Skolnik; and Christian K. Laine of NEOCON.

In creating the catalogue, Harvey Retzloff has proved a most understanding designer and Carl Reisig of Congress Printing, a superb printer. Thanks especially to the loan of a number of computers and the programming skills of Billie McGrew, whose continuous interest in the Project saw it through difficult times and paved the way for a smooth and speedy production of this catalogue. Photography and printing was provided by Ross-Ehlert, Inc., Hedrich Blessing, Cheri Eisenberg, Michael Tropea and Rolf Achilles.

Many individuals and firms have helped by lending material to the exhibition and lending counsel. Among these is Thomas Burleigh, who, through a cache of pictures provided a thorough insight into life at IIT; Jack Hedrich of Hedrich Blessing; and Ivan Zaknic of John Burgee Architects with Philip Johnson; Norman Ross and the many students who lent slides of their professional work.

We are particularly grateful to the Graham Foundation for Advanced Studies in the Fine Arts; the National Endowment for the Humanities; the Illinois Arts Council, a state agency; Phyllis Lambert; the Illinois Institute of Technology; numerous foundations and individuals for their generous financial support.

Mies van der Rohe Centennial Project

FOREWORD

As the institution that invited Mies in 1937 to establish his innovative curriculum in its Department of Architecture and then supported him throughout his tenure as chairman and beyond, the Illinois Institute of Technology is honored by giving recognition to Mies's contribution to architectural education with this Centennial celebration of Mies as Educator. Our endeavors are, of course, reinforced by many other books, lectures and exhibitions around the world, all directed to a better understanding of this architectural greatness so close to us in history. And yet, what is the lesson to be learned?

For me, it is to be reminded of an exceptional generation of architects at the turn of the century who responded to a world of dynamic social change and accelerating technology and then to view Mies's struggle to clarify a meaningful architecture within this context. Instilled from childhood with a strong sense of craftsmanship and the heritage of timeless building materials, his will to learn motivated him to leave Aachen in 1905 at the age of 19 and move to Berlin where he apprenticed with the leading designers and architects of the day. For approximately the next 25 years, the interaction with his peers, his theoretical study of prototypes and the significance of Mies's own buildings produced an architecture that was widely recognized for both its simplicity and beauty.

But most important to our Centennial is that his self-education produced strong convictions about what he felt were basic principles of architecture. These he later translated into an educational program.

It was his unrelenting search for a new architecture that would evolve the thought process of understanding what architecture should be and the related appropriate method of professional education. When Mies became Director of the Bauhaus in 1930, this school, famous for its teaching process of uniting art and technology, was reorganized into a curriculum of architectural education. The knowledge base required for the practice of architecture, including an understanding of materials, structural engineering, heating and ventilating, cost estimating, comparative study of buildings and practical training in the workshops, became the prerequisite for the advanced architecture seminar taught by Mies.

Here, for perhaps the first time, the early years of learning the required professional training and technical skills were combined with the senior experience of developing refined advanced level architectural projects and the study of architecture as an art. After the forced closing of the Bauhaus in 1933, it was Mies's continuing concern with education which led to the opportunity of moving to Chicago and what was to become his architectural destiny.

When offered the directorship of the Department of Architecture at the then Armour Institute he accepted, subject to administration approval of his new program. Developed in Germany, refined in New York and adopted in Chicago, the expanded curriculum truly represented Mies's philosophy of architecture. Submitted as a vertical diagram, entitled 'Program for Architectural Education,' it itemized components of architectural education which are as valid today as they were fifty years ago.

This new curriculum was first implemented during the fall of 1938. During World War II, reduced enrollment permitted the content to be patiently fine-tuned while at the same time Mies was also developing the planning and architecture for the new Illinois Institute of Technology campus. The post-war program was expanded to five years and accredited by the National Architectural Accrediting Board.

Mies's goal as educator was to establish a curriculum concentrating on those areas of architectural education which could be taught. His role as teacher was to work directly with the advanced student. At this level the teaching of architecture and the practice of architecture became one because his buildings represented and, in fact, demonstrated the same principles taught at the school.

The curriculum is structured as if it were a building or, more appropriately, architecture. Carefully sequenced and fully articulated, each learning experience builds: always from the simple to the complex.

The educational objective is to give each student a disciplined method of work and problem solving based on acquiring the significant knowledge and skills of the profession. During the first three years, the student begins by developing drawing ability and visual perception, progressing through Construction as an understanding of principles, acquiring the technical knowledge of related Engineering and studying Function as a way of understanding problems and building types. These three years of comprehensive background are then applied to the development of advanced architectural projects which explore more detailed spatial and visual considerations thus making the fourth and fifth years the synthesis of all previous work. Underlying each of these student problems is the motivation to achieve an optimum level of quality as a fundamental tenet of good architecture.

The faculty is unified by a conviction in both the method and philosophy of this architectural program. Yet, there is always the constant reminder that these ideas, fostered with freshness and creativity, not become dogma. It was never intended that the curriculum become a formula for providing answers, but rather a matrix sensitive to adaptability.

To many who view the brick studies, the work represents only the unrelenting discipline of drawing brick after brick — two lines for each joint. They see only the surface. Yet, the principle of brick bonding, when fully understood, is a building material system having an order and a logic with almost unlimited possibilities. Moreover, this same methodology and understanding can be applied to the problem solving of any new construction technology or building material. When extended throughout the curriculum, this philosophy of teaching Principle instills in each student an ability to make independent decisions. The challenge of both faculty and students is to continually test this theory with the application to actual projects. This process is essential to the vitality of the curriculum and its relevance to current architectural issues. Within the broad range of architectural education IIT represents an academic tradition consistent with today's technology and appropriate for our time.

It is in this spirit that we honor Mies's contribution to architectural education and begin his second hundred years.

George Schipporeit
Project Director
Mies van der Rohe Centennial Project
Dean
College of Architecture, Planning and Design

Reyner Banham, an architectural historian, is a Professor at the University of California, Santa Cruz. His many books include *Theory and Design in the First Machine Age* and *Age of the Masters*.

Fritz Neumeyer, an architectural historian, is an Associate Professor of the History and Theory of Architecture at the Technische Universtät, Berlin. He recently published *Mies van der Rohe — Das kunstlose Wort: Gedanken zur Baukunst*.

Richard Padovan lives in England. He worked as an architect for 15 years and has taught extensively in England and on the Continent. He now writes mainly on Modernism and has recently translated Dom Hans van der Laan's *Architectonic Space*.

Sandra Honey is an architect and architectural historian living in Harare, Zimbabwe. Her articles on Mies have been widely published.

Kevin Harrington teaches architectural history at IIT where he is an Associate Professor. Earlier he published *Changing Ideas on Architecture in the Encyclopedie, 1750-1776*. He is currently at work on a study of the IIT Campus.

THE MASTER OF HUMANE ARCHITECTURE

Reyner Banham

Where now is Ludwig Mies van der Rohe, the humanitarian who taught his students to concern themselves over the convenient design of baggage claim areas and the comfortable height of door handles? Where now Mies the humanist who could quote the Fathers of the Church in the original Latin and taught his students to know and love the great periods of architecture's history? Where, too, is Mies the humane pedagogue who sought to discover his students' strengths and lacks, and taught them to use their own eyes, trust their own judgment?

It is almost as if that kind of Mies van der Rohe had never existed, never taught at the Bauhaus and Illinois Institute of Technology. The world seems bent on remembering only some legendary master of relentless rationalism, the rigid exponent of a single structural system who crushed all clients and students into one invariable procrustean building type. For this, no doubt, his success has been largely to blame, and for the ease with which the superficialities of his classic buildings could be imitated almost everywhere without any understanding of what lay behind them. And, too, his successors may have seemed too much mere followers, continuing a grand educational program whose parts and procedures they had not helped to forge, but were nevertheless loath to change because they had received these lessons of the master as revealed truth.

Even more, perhaps, it is that striving for perfection that informed his own work and was inculcated in all those who came under his direct influence, IIT students included. The object of some early student exercise might be, for instance, to draw a perfect line or set of lines, true, parallel and precise. Every student who by diligence and determination eventually mastered this demanding discipline would, of course, treasure the sheet of paper on which that perfect line was finally drawn, rejecting all others. That sheet would be proudly flourished at family and friends, enshrined in the portfolio that was shown to other schools and prospective employers, and if it survived, stood a fair chance of being reproduced in articles about IIT or the future of architectural education.

And as an illustration of the Miesian method of architectural education it would be delusion, a deception. For it was only a testimony that the exercise had been completed — the actual educational process, the real learning that made a Mies student a Mies student, was what was recorded on all those previous sheets of paper, the rejected versions, the smudges and broken pencil points, the blots and tear stains even. There is coffee and midnight oil involved here, as well as those materials of the drafting table that Mies's students were taught to employ so meticulously — not to mention the advice, consciously sought or gratuitously given, and the commentary, benign or satirical, of practically everyone else in the studio, including the teacher.

The architectural profession is too apt to judge the quality of its educational institutions solely by end products and not by processes — hence all those conversations, and not just at IIT, on the lines of "What happened to old whats-his-face? You never hear about him now but he was a brilliant student." Alas, he may merely have been brilliant at drawing perfect lines, and performing other studio party pieces, and never understood the process by which he acquired that skill. A great teacher does not mistake drawing skills for education and — more importantly

— sees to it that the students never confuse them either. But the outsider looking only at the end products of the work done at IIT might well be misled. The more nearly perfect they were, the better they concealed the human drama, the intellectual progress, that lay behind the achievement.

But in any field of creative activity, a discipline totally mastered is the essential support of the ability to create at liberty, the secure vehicle of fantasy. For Mies, as for most of the great teachers of architecture, this mastery of drawing was also a kind of analogy for the whole process of learning. "We learn to keep our paper clean and our pencil sharp," he would say with the hint of a wink, as if implying that a whole pedagogy of architecture was in that saying; something about keeping our understanding uncluttered and our critical faculties finely honed, no doubt, though Mies's utterances always seemed hermetic or oblique, enough to be open to various readings, almost like those of the great masters of Zen philosophy.

It is a classic Zen paradox that only absolute subjection to an unforgiving discipline can justify the demand to be free, "First acquire a faultless technique, then forget it . . . " was a favorite Zen quotation of Walter Gropius, Mies's predecessor at the Bauhaus. But there is no Mies story that ends with the classic Zen *envoi* "the master struck him and passed on," for Mies was gentle in his ruthlessness, yet his pedagogic method must often have seemed equally gnomic. He rarely corrected a student's work (or that of assistants in his office) or showed them how a design should be done better. Rather, he told them in front of their drawings that something would not work, that a better solution to this or that was needed. The rest was up to them to discover or work out. They were not alone or without help, however. In the big single volume of S.R. Crown Hall, without partitions or hierarchy (other than the sequential location of the five-year cohorts of students) everybody's business was everybody else's business — or could be. The accumulated wisdom and experience of each year above was handily available to each year below, to be tapped by observation, discussion or intellectual osmosis. By processes analogous to the discipline of continuous self-improvement learned in the drawing classes, better solutions were found — self-evidently better in the eyes of the students themselves.

But only, that is, if they had the mental capacities to understand and apply the lessons of the discipline. That was the method at the heart of the gnomic discourse of the studio, and for those who failed to grasp the method (and there were many, as there always will be) there was the very considerable consolation that they had at least acquired such formidable drawing skills that they were instantly employable almost anywhere. And furthermore, they had been very thoroughly schooled in the processes of assembly of a repertoire of modest buildings out of a closely prescribed range of materials, from wood and brick to steel and glass. The repertoire may have been as small as the buildings were modest and the materials restricted, but here again, extension to other scales and materials were available to any student smart enough to draw an analogy.

Somewhere in all this, Mies seems to have rediscovered something like the kernel of the true substance of studio teaching as originally elaborated at the *Ecole des Beaux-Arts*. As every genuine product of the *Ecole* has tirelessly insisted, what went on in studio was drawing as an instrument of education, but that the education only really started when the master seized upon one particular student's project and made it the instance of a *discours sur le methode* for all the rest of the studio to hear and — hopefully — to understand. Mies's discourse was less prolix (to put it mildly) than that of the great professors at the *Ecole*, and for that reason more to be treasured. If remembered fragments of this kind of discourse became lodged permanently in the minds of students of the *Ecole des Beaux-Arts*, how much more true it was of the students from IIT; maxims were recalled and trotted out in later years, in and out of context. Out of context, of course, they were almost incomprehensible even to IIT graduates. Because they seemed so opaque to other understanding, they were usually glossed by references to the aphorisms of Mies's "Inaugural" lecture of 1938, or the categories of the formal curriculum of IIT. Thus, "we might do that when we build on the moon" (apparently first uttered without further explication) seems to have been paired in memory with the opening phrase of the Inaugural "All education must begin with the practical side of life" and taken to mean that it was not practicable to whatever that was here on Earth.

But Mies *might* have meant a number of other things by this quip. Carrying back observations, made impromptu about particular designs, into the measured cadences and diagrammatic clarity of formal documents, can lead to "understandings" that can be total hogwash, and there are good reasons for this. One is that official philosophies of architecture schools are essentially ceremonial documents; they describe all sorts of important topics and attitudes, some almost

Furthermore, since according to Aquinas "our intellect is not directly capable of knowing anything that is not universal," it follows that the work of art, the man made thing, is more directly and completely knowable than natural things. Originating from an infinite and un-created intelligence, they cannot be fully apprehended by our finite created intellect; but the man made thing, which originates in that finite intellect, embodies the rational and universal forms of human thought, and is directly intelligible. Compared with the endless nuances, sub-tleties and complexities of nature, art appears crude and primitive; but for the intellect it has a special immediacy and clarity. Maritain writes in *Art and Scholasticism* that:

...in the beauty which has been termed connatural to man and is peculiar to human art this brilliance of form, however purely intelligible it may be in itself, is apprehended in the sensible and by the sensible, and not separately from it.... The mind then, spared the least effort of abstraction, rejoices without labor and without discussion. It is excused its customary task, it has not to extricate something intelligible from the matter in which it is buried and then step by step go through its various attributes; like the stag at the spring of running water, it has nothing to do but drink, and it drinks the clarity of being.[10]

Thanks to their intelligibility, man made things can act as necessary intermediaries between us and the natural world, bringing to it an added radiance, such as a Greek temple brings to the landscape in which it is set. It is as though nature demanded the clear sharp facets of our rational creations for its own completion; Mies observed that:

We must strive to bring nature, buildings and men together in a higher unity. When you see nature through the glass walls of the Farnsworth house, it takes on a deeper significance than when you stand outside. Thus nature becomes more expressive — it becomes part of a greater whole.

Much adverse criticism of Mies's work and philosophy has been based on the misconception that they were founded on a Platonist belief in a transcendental world of universal essences, of which his buildings were intended as symbols. Thus Mumford complains in "The Case Against Modern Architecture" that "these hollow glass shells...existed alone in the Platonic world of his imagination..."[12] while Jencks, in *Modern Movements in Architecture*, fails to distinguish between Plato and Aquinas:

The problem of Mies van der Rohe...is that he demands an absolute commit-ment to the Platonic world-view in order to appreciate his buildings.... For instance, nominalist philosophers and pragmatists, who believe that universals

do not in fact exist, would find the Platonic statements of Mies mostly just humorous, because they go to such terrific pains to project a nonexistent reality.... Not only does Mies refer to Aquinas's formulation explicitly, but he also seems to uphold the further scholastic doctrine that all the apparent phenomena of this world are actually mere symbols for a greater reality lying behind them.[13]

On the contrary, for Aquinas, and likewise for Mies, things are not mere appearances or symbols but real, while universals exist only in the intellect. Mies's architecture does not aim at universality in order to symbolize a platonic world of ideal Forms, but simply in order to be intelligible. Its whole intent is to state, as lucidly as it can, what it is and how it is made. This fundamental matter-of-factness, this *Sachlichkeit*, was underlined by Ernesto Rogers in *Casabella*:

Obviously, when Mies cites St. Augustine's phrase "Beauty is the splendor of truth" he cannot take refuge in the metaphysical halo of the great Saint, because Mies's truth is neither revealed, nor aprioristic, nor in the strict philosophical sense objective.... Mies's religion is that of a layman who has an existential limit, and it is only in the affirmation of the real, historically understood, that he can satisfy his craving for truth, and thereby for beauty.[14]

Moreover, the "reductivism" of which Mies's critics accuse him is not a denial of the richness and complexity of nature, but intended to accen-tuate it:

Nature too must lead its own life. We should take care not to disturb it with the colorfulness of our houses and interiors.[15]

The Farnsworth house has never I believe been really understood. I myself was in that house from morning to evening. Up to then I had not known how beautiful the colors in nature can be. One must deliberately use neutral tones in interiors, because one has every color outside. These colors change continuously and completely, and I have to say that simplicity is splendid.[16]

The striving for structural clarity, and for that "splendid simplicity" which found fulfillment in the Farnsworth House, was confirmed by Mies's reading of Aquinas; but it had at first to contend with other influences that pulled in opposite directions. The image built up in the hagiographies of the 1960's, of the granite monolith impervious to the battles that were going on around him, is one-sided. It must be set against the fact that in his German years he was very much "in the thick of it."[17] as Sandra Honey has said, and shared fully in the intellectual conflicts of his time.

Doric Temple, Segesta, Sicily. Late 5th Century B.C. Courtesy of Rolf Achilles.

Ludwig Mies van der Rohe, Farnsworth House, Plano. 1945–50. Courtesy of Hedrich Blessing.

It is impossible to determine how early Aquinas became important for Mies; in Fritz Neumeyer's view it was only in his later years.[18] One can fairly safely rule out any likelihood that he was exposed to Scholastic teachings as a pupil at the Cathedral School at Aachen, as has often been assumed. The anecdote quoted earlier, about his discovery of Aquinas's definition of truth, gives the impression that it happened while he was in Behrens's office (1908–12), but that is unclear. However Schulze cites the recollection of Mies's assistant Friedrich Hirz, who joined him in 1928 when he started work on the Barcelona Pavilion, that "he read a lot of St. Thomas Aquinas" while he was with him.[19] One can reasonably conclude, I think, that Aquinas could have begun to have an influence on Mies's work during the 1920's. Mies's first designs of the 1920's either continue (like the Kempner, Feldmann, Eichstaedt and Mosler houses) the Neoclassicism of his prewar work, or reflect the influence of Expressionism, and above all that of his close friend Hugo Häring, who shared Mies's atelier from 1921 to 1924. This is most evident in the two projects for glass office buildings, of 1921 and 1922. Schulze notes that: "Häring's own project for the Friedrichstrasse competition, which was probably worked out simultaneously with Mies's, is notable for fat, rolling exterior curves that readily bring the undulating volumes of Mies's second project to mind."[20]

What is strikingly absent from both projects is structural clarity. Schulze illustrates a sketch plan of the 1922 skyscraper, describing it as,

a most unconvincing effort, in which a geometric system of piers is forced to take root in the amoeboid plan. The geometry itself collapses into irregularity and all trace of rational order is lost.... In the Glass Skyscraper Mies was preoccupied less with structure than with form.[21]

Writing about the two glass towers in *Frühlicht*, Mies threw in a functional justification of the skyscraper's apparently "arbitrary" curved outline — "sufficient illumination of the interior" — but this is less convincing than his other two reasons: "the massing of the building viewed from the street, and ... the play of reflections."[22]

The design is hard to reconcile with his statements that it was "not the task of architecture to invent form," and "Form is not the aim of our work, but only the result."[23]

1922 seems to have been a turning point in Mies's development. Within a few months of the glass skyscraper, apparently in the winter of 1922-23, he designed the concrete office building. An ideological gulf

separates the two projects; there could be no better starting point for the story I want to trace here: Mies's gradual clarification of the structure of his buildings at the expense, if need be, of all other concerns. He acknowledged the self-denial the intellectual asceticism, that this involved:

I often throw out things I like very much — they are dear to my heart — but when I have a better idea — a *clearer* idea, I mean — then I follow that clearer idea. After a while I found the Washington Bridge most beautiful, the best building in New York, and maybe at the beginning I wouldn't you know. That grew; but first I had to conquer the idea, and later I appreciated it as a beauty. Thomas Aquinas says that "Reason is the first principle of all human work." Now when you have once grasped that, then you act accordingly. So I would throw out everything that is not reasonable. I don't want to be interesting; I want to be good."[24]

Between 1922 and 1962 when he began to work on the National Gallery in Berlin, Mies progressively simplified his plans reducing them finally to a single vast square space, and articulated his structure so that each element was unmistakably distinct from every other. There is a striking, and I believe not merely coincidental, parallel with the development of the classic Gothic style over a similar period of time, about 1190–1230, and under the influence of the same Scholastic demand for *claritas*. Then, too, the linked autonomous spaces of Romanesque were reduced

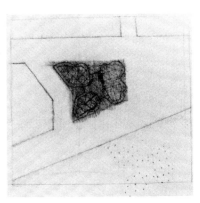

Ludwig Mies van der Rohe, Glass Skyscraper Project, Friedrichstrasse, Berlin. 1922. Sketch of plan. Courtesy of Museum of Modern Art.

Ludwig Mies van der Rohe, Concrete Office Building Project. 1922. Courtesy of Museum of Modern Art.

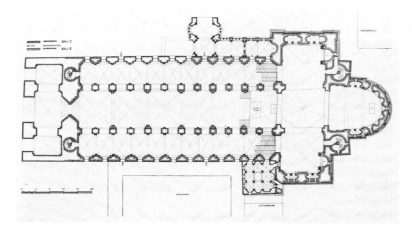

Cathedral, Speyer. Floor Plan of c.1106. Courtesy of Hans Erich Kubach; *Dom zu Speyer*, Darmstadt. 1974. p. 99.

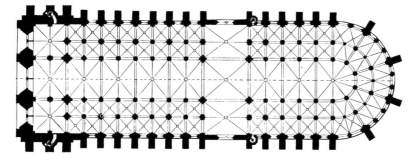

Notre Dame, Paris. Floor Plan of 1163. Courtesy of Andrew Martindale. *Gothic Art*. N.Y., 1967. p. 23.

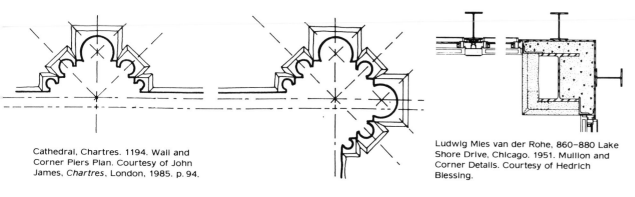

Cathedral, Chartres. 1194. Wall and Corner Piers Plan. Courtesy of John James, *Chartres*, London, 1985. p. 94.

Ludwig Mies van der Rohe, 860–880 Lake Shore Drive, Chicago. 1951. Mullion and Corner Details. Courtesy of Hedrich Blessing.

to the single uniform space of High Gothic; and the structure was articulated so that each member was clearly identified. The classic Miesian corner detail is comparable to the classic Gothic compound pier with its central shaft surrounded by a cluster of slender colonnettes, each corresponding to a separate arch or vault rib. In *Gothic Architecture and Scholasticism* Erwin Panofsky writes:

As High Scholasticism was governed by the principle of *manifestatio*, so was High Gothic architecture dominated by what may be called the "principle of transparence..." Like the High Scholastic *summa*, the High Gothic cathedral aimed, first of all, as "totality" and therefore tended to approximate, by synthesis as well as elimination, one perfect and final solution.... Instead of the Romanesque variety of western and eastern vaulting forms... we have the newly developed rib vault exclusively so that the vaults of even the apse, the chapels and the ambulatory no longer differ in kind from those of the nave and transept....

And:

According to classic Gothic standards the individual elements... must proclaim their identity by remaining clearly separated from each other — shafts from the wall or the core of the pier, the ribs from their neighbors, all vertical members from their arches; and there must be an unequivocal correlation between them.[25]

However neither Mies nor the Gothic builders arrived at the "one perfect and final solution" by a smooth progression. The development of classic Gothic, as Panofsky shows, was consistent, but not direct:

On the contrary, when observing the evolution from the beginning to the "final solutions," we receive the impression that it went on almost after the fashion of a "jumping procession," taking two steps forward and then one backward, as though the builders were deliberately placing obstacles in their own way.[26]

Similarly, one has the feeling that Mies could have gone straight from the concrete office project, the most prophetic of his early projects, to the IIT campus, leaving out all the stages in between; for in it appear all the characteristics of his later work: reduction of the concept to its simplest, most essential statement; clear, regular structure; and universal, omni-functional space. But things are never that simple. Only by being open to contradictory influences, and resolving the resulting conflicts by what Zevi calls "the flagrant dissonances of Barcelona, Berlin and Brno"[27] could Mies have arrived at the truly complex simplicity of the National Gallery.

With the two Country House Projects — in concrete (early 1923) and brick (winter 1923–24) he veers off in a new direction, under the by now

now strong influence of Theo van Doesburg and *De Stijl* through his close involvement with *G*. There was much about *De Stijl* to attract him: here, finally, was a new art movement inspired primarily by philosophy; and its foundation manifesto had declared that the "new consciousness of the age" was "directed towards the universal."[28]

But the philosophical bases of *De Stijl* were closer to Platonism (though it derived from German and Indian philosophy rather than Greek) than to Aquinas's common sense acceptance of the real existence of material things. It aimed at the representation, *beelding*, not of phenomena, but of a noumenal world of pure thought.[29] In painting, this was to be achieved by eliminating the figural *object* and replacing it by a unity of rectangular planes of primary color.[30] In architecture, it would be achieved by eliminating the figural delimitation of *space* — the room clearly defined by four walls or corner columns — and replacing it with a continuous space in which walls and columns stood as isolated planes and lines. Point 5 of Van Doesburg's manifesto *Towards a Plastic Architecture* (1924) declared:

The subdivision of functional spaces is strictly determined by rectangular planes, which... can be imagined extended into infinity, thereby forming a system of coordinates in which all points correspond to an equal number of points in universal, unlimited open space.

Pure thought, in which no representation derived from phenomena is involved, but which instead is based on number, measure, proportion and abstract line, is revealed conceptually (as rationality) in Chinese, Greek and German philosophy, and aesthetically in the Neoplasticism of our time.[31]

Neither the three house projects that Van Doesburg and Van Eesteren showed in the exhibition "Les Architectes du Groupe 'de Styl'," in Paris in October 1923, nor the Rietveld-Schröder House of 1924, succeeded in this aim; the Paris models consisted of intersecting volumes, not planes, the Schröder House, externally, of a rectangular box with Neoplastic surface decoration. Only Mies's second Brick House Project fulfilled Van Doesburg's aims.

However, since the walls were asymmetrically disposed (Point 12 had rejected repetition and symmetry in favor of "the balanced repetition of unequal parts") it was impossible, so long as they remained load-bearing, to achieve a clear structure. Inevitably some walls carried loads and others not, while spans were unequal and varied in direction. Mies's three brick houses of the late 1920's (Wolf, Esters and Lange) are all more practical reworkings of the project; all have living rooms

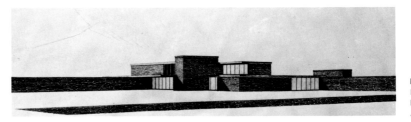

Ludwig Mies van der Rohe, Brick Country House Project. 1922. Perspective Drawing. Courtesy of Museum of Modern Art.

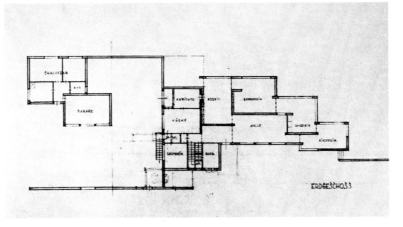

Ludwig Mies van der Rohe, Esters House, Krefeld. 1928. Floor Plan. Courtesy of Museum of Modern Art.

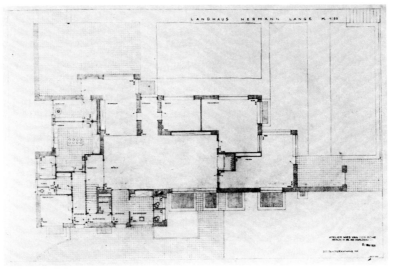

Ludwig Mies van der Rohe, Hermann Lange House, Krefeld. 1928. Floor Plan. Courtesy of Museum of Modern Art.

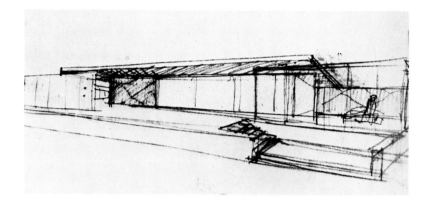

Ludwig Mies van der Rohe, German Pavilion, Barcelona. 1928. Perspective Sketch. Courtesy of Museum of Modern Art.

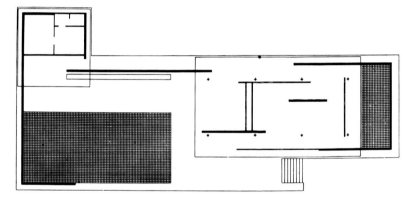

Ludwig Mies van der Rohe, German Pavilion, Barcelona. 1928. Floor Plan, Plan One. Courtesy of Museum of Modern Art.

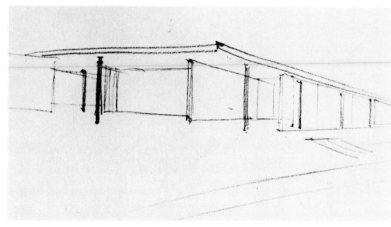

Ludwig Mies van der Rohe, German Pavilion, Barcelona. 1928. Perspective sketch. Courtesy of Museum of Modern Art.

planned as series of overlapping rectangles, producing staggered garden elevations; and all wrestle unsuccessfully with the problem of structural clarity. It took Mies five years to find a solution, though Van Doesburg's Point 8, "Walls are no longer load bearing; they have been reduced to points of support . . . ."[32]

Mies has recalled that in the early days of the Barcelona project, in 1928, that "One evening as I was working late on the building I made a sketch of a freestanding wall, and I got a shock. I knew it was a new principle."[33] This was the birth of the onyx wall that formed the core of the Pavilion. Yet why did it constitute a new principle? He had used freestanding walls, in the sense of isolated planes in space, in the country house project; what was new could only be the idea that the wall stood free of the structure, and loads were carried by columns. The columns were slow to appear, however; the earliest surviving plans and sketches show quite recognizable versions of the design, with overhanging roof slab, two courts containing pools, and a plinth approached by steps; but no columns. Then, late in 1928, they finally appear; but at first there are three rows, and their arrangement looks irregular. A later plan shows two rows, but of three columns only, one end of the roof still being supported by walls. Finally, a completely regular structure and freely composed wall planes are superposed as independent but contrapuntal systems. It is as though the concrete office building and the brick country house had been overlaid — a synthesis of Scholasticist clarity and Neoplasticist spatial continuity.

Just as Mies's brick houses of the 1920's reworked the project of 1923–24, the houses of the 1930's were variations on the Barcelona theme. But by 1945–46, when Mies began to design the Farnsworth House, this synthesis was no longer good (that is, clear) enough. The rationality of the Pavilion's structure was apparent only in plan; in three dimensions, the structural bay defined by four columns was nowhere visible. The walls played an ambiguous role, threatening to usurp that of the columns. (Sandra Honey has reported [34] that they in fact concealed a further five supplementary columns; it is hard to see what purpose these served, other than lateral bracing.)

The Barcelona Pavilion, the Farnsworth House and the unbuilt Bacardi Project (first formulation, if one excludes the Fifty by Fifty House and Convention Hall projects, of the "perfect and final solution" of the Berlin Gallery) form as it were a set. Each consists of a pavilion raised above ground level, approached off axis by flights of steps and supported by eight columns; each marks a breakthrough in Mies's search for clarity; and each is the model for subsequent designs. At Plano, the ambiguities of Barcelona are overcome by bringing the columns to the outer edge of the roof and floor planes and stopping all interior divisions short of the ceiling; for Bacardi, the plan is reduced to a single great bay, with two columns on each side. Less is more. As happened in the 1920's and 30's, the theme, once stated, is repeated. The Farnsworth House becomes the model for S. R. Crown Hall, the Mannheim Theatre and the Bacardi Building in Mexico City; the unbuilt Bacardi project, for the Schaefer Museum and the Berlin Gallery.

Thus Mies's career proceeded dialectically, like the articles in Aquinas's *Summa*, in which he sets one argument (*videtur quod*) against another (*sed contra*) and proceeds to a solution (*respondeo dicendum*). It was not, as Zevi describes, a parabola with its summit around 1930, so much as a series of fluctuations with an ultimate goal — like the twisting course of a river which at last must flow into the sea. And (to pursue the simile) just as a river bears down to the sea sediment from its upper reaches, so, without the Brick Country House Project, the Barcelona Pavilion and the Farnsworth House, Mies's final statement, the Berlin Gallery, would not have been possible.

Aquinas's phrase may also help to answer the two most common criticisms raised against Mies's work: that despite all the talk about truth, his buildings are in fact false in their expression of structure; and that they make intolerable demands on those who live in them. The first is based chiefly on his practice, at Lake Shore Drive and elsewhere, of cladding the concrete casing of his steel columns with steel plates, and then applying to them I-section mullions which support no glazing. (The hidden columns at Barcelona would fall into the same category).

But Aquinas defined truth as a *correspondence between different things*, or between thing and intellect and not as an identity. The steel facings of Mies's columns correspond to the steel within, in the same way as the abstract concept of the thing understood by the intellect corresponds, but is not identical, to the material individuality of the thing itself. Aquinas himself answered the objection that "the intellect is false if it understands an object otherwise than as it really is" by distinguishing between false abstraction, which considers the form of a thing *as being separate* from its matter — as Plato held — and true abstraction, which merely considers the form of the thing *separately* from its matter, "according to the mode of the intellect, and not materially,

according to the mode of a material thing."[35] Similarly, the visible steel structure at Lake Shore Drive is necessary to make the real steel structure manifest; it does not try to present that structure as being otherwise than it really is. Panofsky sees the same "visual logic" in the classic Gothic cathedral:

We are faced neither with "rationalism" in a purely functionalistic sense nor with "illusion" in the modern sense of *l'art pour l'art* aesthetics. We are faced with what may be termed a "visual logic" illustrative of Thomas Aquinas's *nam et sensus ratio quaedam est*. A man imbued with the Scholastic habit would look upon the mode of architectural presentation . . . from the point of view of *manifestatio*. He would have taken it for granted that the primary purpose of the many elements that compose a cathedral was to ensure stability, just as he took it for granted that the primary purpose of the many elements that constitute a *Summa* was to ensure validity. But he would not have been satisfied had not the membrification of the edifice permitted him to re-experience the very processes of architectural composition just as the membrification of the *Summa* permitted him to re-experience the very processes of cogitation.[36]

The second criticism, which is more fundamental and is the reason for my title, has been leveled against Mies since early in his career. In 1931 *Die Form* the organ of the *Deutscher Werkbund* whose vice-president Mies became in 1926, published an article under the title "Can one live in the Tugendhat house?" The author, Justus Bier, claimed that "personal life was repressed" by the "precious" spaces and furnishing of the house, making it a "showroom" rather than a home.[37] In the mid-1960's Mumford said much the same:

these hollow glass shells . . . had no relation to site, climate, insulation, function, or internal activity, [and] the rigidly arranged chairs in his living rooms openly disregarded the necessary intimacies and informalities of conversation;[38]

and Venturi, that "Mies's exquisite pavilions . . . ignore the real complexity and contradiction inherent in the domestic program."[39]

Even Mies's biographer, Franz Schulze, recognizes that the Farnsworth House,

is more nearly a temple than a dwelling, and it rewards aesthetic contemplation before it fulfills domestic necessity . . . . In cold weather the great glass panes tended to accumulate an overabundance of condensation . . . In summer . . . the sun turned the interior into a cooker . . . Palumbo is the ideal owner of the house . . . he derives sufficient spiritual sustenance from the reductivist beauty of the place to endure its creature discomforts.[40]

Of course that is just the point; Mies's buildings, before they are functional shelters or even objects of "aesthetic contemplation," are sources

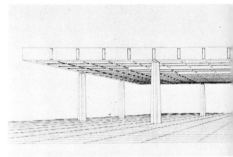

Ludwig Mies van der Rohe, Bacardi Office Building Project, Santiago de Cuba. 1957. Perspective of Structure. Courtesy of Fritz Neumeyer.

Ludwig Mies van der Rohe, New National Gallery, Berlin. 1967. Courtesy of Werner Blaser.

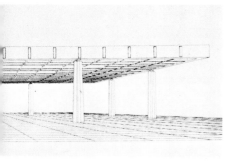

Le Corbusier, Pavillon de l'Esprit
Nouveau. 1925. From *Oeuvre Complete
de 1910–1929*, Zurich. 1964. p. 107.

Ludwig Mies van der Rohe, Tugendhat
House, Brno. 1930. Courtesy of George
Danforth.

of "spiritual sustenance" — that is, of food for the mind. It is instructive
to compare Mies's attitude in this respect with that of Le Corbusier, who
seems to have agreed, in theory if not in practice, with Loos's dictum
that:

Only a very small part of architecture belongs to art: the tomb and the monument. Everything else, everything which serves a purpose, should be excluded
from the realms of art.[41]

James Dunnett has recently argued that:

The Radiant City . . . was to be a setting for a particular ideal of intellectual life, the
model of which was, above all, that of Cubism — which for Le Corbusier was
essentially a meditative art . . . . In describing the house as a "machine for living
in" Le Corbusier was classifying it according to a principle of differentiation
which was central to his thought and to his sense of form . . . . The division
opposed the essentially "servant" functions of life and the "free" functions . . . . [It]
was extended to the field of artefacts by recognizing two distinct categories: the
"free" artefact, i.e. the work of art, and the "servant" artefact, i.e. the implement
or tool (*outil*). Though the former needed no ulterior justification, the latter was
justified only by its service to the processes of life, and hence to the enjoyment,
ultimately, of the former . . . . The role of a "machine for living in" is *outillage* —
that of servant.[42]

In classifying the house as a machine or tool Le Corbusier was regarding it not as a work of art — a proper object of meditation in itself — but
rather as the self-effacing container of that proper object, namely the
Cubist painting. Its role was to be "a vessel of silence and lofty solitude"
in which the work of art could be meditated upon.[43]

Of course Mies's houses, too, could enhance the experience of a work of
art, despite Justus Bier's objection that one could not hang pictures in
the main space of the Tugendhat House. But their intention went beyond that: to the enhancement of the experience of life itself. Replying in
Die Form to Bier's criticisms, Grete Tugendhat observed:

I have . . . never felt the spaces to be precious, but rather as austere and grand —
not in a way that oppresses, however, so much as one that liberates . . . . Just as in
this space one sees each flower as never before, and every work of art (for
instance the sculpture that stands before the onyx wall) speaks more strongly, so
too the human occupant stands out, for himself and others, more distinctly from
his environment.[44]

For Mies, as for Le Corbusier, the house was a machine a *méditer*. But
where for Le Corbusier it was merely a machine to meditate *in*, for Mies
it was a machine to meditate *with*. An educator could have no higher
aim.

25

NOTES

1 Werner Blaser, *Mies van der Rohe, Furniture and Interiors*, 1980, p. 10.
2 Peter Carter, *Architectural Design*, March 1961, p. 97.
3 Franz Schulze, *Mies van der Rohe: A Critical Biography*, Chicago: University of Chicago Press, 1985, p. 173.
4 Schulze, p. 313.
5 St. Thomas Aquinas, *Quaestiones disputatae de veritate*, 1256-59, part I qu. 86, art. 2, translation author.
6 St. Thomas Aquinas, *Summa Theologica*, 1267, part I qu. 86, art. 1, 1267, translation 1st 2 lines, Anthony Kenny, *Aquinas*, Oxford: Oxford University Press, 1980; 2nd two lines, Fathers of the Dominican Province, translators, Aquinas, *Summa*, London & Chicago: Burns Oates & Washbourne, 1922.
7 Aquinas, *De veritate*, qu. I art. 3.
8 Aquinas, *De veritate*, qu. I art. 2.
9 Aquinas, *De veritate*, qu. XX art. 4.
10 Jacques Maritain, *Art and Scholasticism*, 1923.
11 Christian Norberg-Schulz, "Ein Gespräch mit Mies van der Rohe," *Baukunst und Werkform*, Nov. 1958.
12 Lewis Mumford, "The Case Against Modern Architecture," *Architectural Record*, 1962.
13 Charles Jencks, *Modern Movements in Architecture*, 1973, pp. 95-108.
14 E. Rogers, "Problematica di Mies van der Rohe," *Casabella*, 214, Feb.-Mar. 1957, p. 6.
15 Norberg-Schulz
16 Ludwig Mies van der Rohe, "Ich mache niemals ein Bild," *Bauwelt*, Aug. 1962.
17 Sandra Honey, "The Office of Mies van der Rohe in America," *UIA International Architect*, issue 3, 1984, p. 44.
18 Conversation with Neumeyer.
19 Schulze, p. 338, note 43.
20 Schulze, p. 103.
21 Schulze, p. 101.
22 Mies, "Two Glass Skyscrapers," *Frühlicht*, Summer 1922.
23 Mies, *G*, number 2, 1923.
24 Mies, "Conversations about the Future of Architecture," Reynolds Metals Company sound recording, 1958.
25 Erwin Panofsky, *Gothic Architecture and Scholasticism*, Latrobe, Pennsylvania: The Archabbey Press, 1951, pp.43-50.
26 Panofsky, p. 60.
27 Bruno Zevi, *Poetica dell'architettura neoplastica*, 2nd edition, 1974, p. 187.
28 1st manifesto of De Stijl, *De Stijl*, II. 1, 1918, p. 2.
29 Theo van Doesburg, "Denken-aanschouwen-beelden," *De Stijl*, II. 2, 1918, p. 23.
30 Piet Mondrian, "De nieuwe beelding in de schilderkunst 3," *De Stijl*, I. 4, 1918, p. 29.
31 Theo van Doesburg, "Tot een beeldende architectuur," *De Stijl*, VI. 6/7, 1924, pp. 78-83.
32 van Doesburg, "Tot een beeldende architectuur."
33 Mies, *Six Students Talk with Mies*, North Carolina State College, Spring 1952.
34 Sandra Honey, "Who and What Inspired Mies van der Rohe in Germany," *Architectural Design*, 3/4, 1979, p.102.
35 Aquinas, *Summa Theologica*, part I, qu. 85, art. 1.
36 Panofsky, pp. 58-59.
37 Justus Bier, "Kann man im Haus Tugendhat wohnen?" *Die Form*, Oct. 1931, pp. 392-393.
38 Mumford, "The Case Against Modern Architecture."
39 Robert Venturi, *Complexity and Contradiction in Architecture*, 1966, pp. 24-25.
40 Schulze, p. 256.
41 Adolf Loos, *Architecture*, 1910.
42 James Dunnett, "The Architecture of Silence," *The Architectural Review*, Oct 1985, pp. 69-75.
43 Le Corbusier, *La ville radieuse*, 1935.
44 Grete Tugendhat, "Die Bewohner des Hauses Tugendhats äussern sich," *Die Form*, Nov. 1931, pp. 437-38.

MIES AS SELF-EDUCATOR

Fritz Neumeyer

"Formula of my Happiness: a Yes, a No, a straight line, *a goal*."
— Friedrich Nietzsche

"My father was a stone mason, so it was natural that I would either continue his work or turn to building. I had no conventional architectural education. I worked under a few good architects; I read a few good books — and that's about it."[1]

With this, the essence of a "biography," Mies van der Rohe marked those specific moments which defined his professional path from material to function to idea. What Mies may have learned from those specific forms of construction known since childhood can be gleaned from Adolph Loos. Also a stone mason's son Loos wrote in his famous essay "Architektur" of 1909, "only a very small portion of architecture is art: the tombstone and the monument. Everything else which serves a function is to be excluded from the realm of art. Only when the colossal misunderstanding that art is something adapted to a function is overcome will we have the architecture of our time."[2]

Mies came in contact early with this small yet extremely important aspect of architecture, belonging as it does to the resources of a stone mason. Tombstones and monuments embodied an absolute ideal as well as a formal step beyond architecture. This served not only to acquaint him with the practical side of construction but also to sensitize him to the quality of material and uniform character of what was built. The metaphysical was its essence of reality, symbolic nature its actual being, for its function was to transcend visible physical reality by referring to the numinous world of the invisible.

During these student years in Aachen another encounter occurred, which Mies claimed to be of lasting significance. Cleaning out the drawer of a drafting table in the office of Aachen architect Albert Schneider, where Mies worked briefly, he found an issue of *Die Zukunft* (The Future), published by Maximilian Harden. Reading it with great interest, Mies later admitted[3] that the content of this journal far surpassed his understanding, yet awakened his curiosity and concern. From then on Mies considered questions of philosophy and culture; he read intensively and began to think for himself.[4]

This chance encounter with the Berlin weekly *Die Zukunft*, which he now read regularly, brought Mies into contact with a hitherto unfamiliar world. A megaphone of anti-Wilhelminian rebellion, known as the most read, most admired and most hated political weekly in Germany, presented to its turn of the century readers such well known writers as the art critics Karl Scheffler, Julius Meier-Graefe and Alfred Lichtwark, the Danish literature scholar George Brandes and the Berlin historian Kurt Breysig. Author-artists such as Henry van de Velde and August Endell, writers of fiction such as Richard Dehmel, Stefan Zweig, Heinrich Mann or August Strindberg, the economic historian Werner Sombart and the philosophers Alois Riehl and Georg Simmel rounded out the list of contributors.

Acquaintance with this journal had weighty potential significance. Issue no. 52, September 27, 1902, seems almost a prophecy of Mies's future as it contained an essay by Alois Riehl "From Heraclitus to Spinoza," and a report by Meier-Graef on the Art Exposition of Turin where the vestibule designed by Peter Behrens caused a sensation.

Mies would not meet Alois Riehl and Peter Behrens until five years later in Berlin, where they profoundly influenced his intellectual and artistic development. The religiously biased education Mies received at The Cathedral School in Aachen planted a special disposition for the absolute and metaphysical and a tendency towards a comparable world view. This tendency took firm root following his chance encounter with philosophy in *Die Zukunft*. In 1927 Mies wrote in his notebook, "Only through philosophical understanding is the correct order of our duties revealed and thereby the value and dignity of our existence."[5]

For Mies the key to reality lay hidden in philosophical understanding. Philosophy, alone among the paths to enlightenment, had the advantage of depth and simplicity, because its method separated the primary from the secondary, the eternal from the temporal. Mies sought in his study of philosophy an intellectual equivalent to his lack of academic training as an architect. "Reduction" to the essence offered "the only way," to genuine understanding and the possibility "to create important architecture."[6]

This intellectual premise had a personal counterpart, for Mies's first step into architectural independence grew from his interest in philosophy. He built his first house in 1907, his twenty-first year, for a philosopher. At the time, Mies worked for Bruno Paul. In addition to his work, Mies attended the courses Bruno Paul taught at the Berlin Museum for Applied Arts. Here Mies had his first important artistic experiences and learned from the elegance of Paul's design.

Building the house for Alois Riehl, Professor of Philosophy at The Friedrich Wilhelm University in Berlin, introduced Mies in 1907 into the world he had first encountered in reading *Die Zukunft*. His first patron, a close friend until his death in 1924 and for whom Mies designed his tombstone, provided a decisive entrance into that strata of society, primarily intellectuals, artists, businessmen, industrialists and financiers, from which Mies later received commissions. In this cosmopolitan world of Berlin, Mies met at the Riehl house Walther Rathenau, the classical philologist Werner Jaeger, the art historian Heinrich Wölfflin (then engaged to Ada Bruhn, she married Mies in 1913), the philosopher Eduard Spranger and probably also the philosopher of religion, Romano Guardini, who influenced Mies's thinking of the late twenties. The Riehl House shows the first influences of classicism Mies absorbed from the Berlin building tradition. Thoroughly modern in its contemporary interpretation of sober Biedermeier publicized in 1907 by Paul

Ludwig Mies van der Rohe seated in front of the Riehl House. 1912. Courtesy of Franz Schulze.

Ludwig Mies van der Rohe, Riehl House, Neubabelsberg. 1907. Garden view. Courtesy of *Moderne Bauformen*, 1910.

Mebes in his influential *Bauen um 1800* (Building Around 1800), even more important than stylistic surface considerations, Mies mastered the grammar of the composition. By overlapping volumes of geometric form, also expressed in the tense plan, Mies's signature becomes clear.

Bruno Paul, Clubhouse of the Berlin Lawn and Tennis Club. c.1908. Courtesy of Fritz Neumeyer.

Peter Behrens, Crematorium in Hagen. 1906–07. Courtesy of Fritz Hoeber, *Peter Behrens*, Munich, 1913. p.64.

Peter Behrens, Atelier in Potsdam, Neubabelsberg. Mies is third from right. Courtesy of A.E.G. Archive.

Peter Behrens, A.E.G. Turbine Hall, Berlin-Moabit. 1909. Courtesy of A.E.G. Archive.

Behind the *Bieder* or honest appearance of the entry shell Mies selected for this house, he treated the garden facade as a pavilion set asymmetrically on a monumental base — a theme he followed to the end of his life. If, in the mind's eye, one removed from this house everything but the pilasters of the walls and the loggia, the structure seems to suggest the Farnsworth House or the National Gallery, Berlin. The pavilion is probably the first architectural exercise Mies addressed in Berlin. Not only

Schinkel's buildings in nearby Potsdam, but also Paul's Club House of the Berlin Lawn and Tennis Club in Zehlendorf, show concepts on which the Riehl House draws. Paul entrusted Mies with the planning of the Zehlendorf building, and it thus numbers among his first works. While working for Bruno Paul, Mies became familiar with the works of Peter Behrens especially his 1906 crematorium in Hagen, which also may have influenced the plan of the Riehl House. Paul Thiersch, Mies's supervisor in Paul's office, worked on the crematorium in 1906 while in Behrens's office in Düsseldorf. Recognizing his talent Thiersch told Mies that "you belong with Behrens."[7]

The Berlin office of Peter Behrens, who in 1907 became artistic adviser to the international electrical conglomerate A.E.G., offered a spectrum of work unmatched by any other architectural office in Europe of the time. His concept of a synthesis of art and life in a grand uniform style expressed itself in a distinct industrial classicism where opposing worlds of industrial technology and ceremonial art were reconciled. The renowned Turbine Hall of 1909 symbolized a new aesthetic power, which promised to overcome the stylistic pluralism of the 19th century. Behrens's "Zarathustra Style," as a contemporary art critic termed it, announced the "Kunstwollen" (will to art) which Riegl's art theory had first proclaimed. In it one heard the echo of the "will to a great style" as postulated by the philosopher Friedrich Nietzsche in his thesis on the dominance of art over life. Only in art could man regain his lost wholeness. An attempt to organize a new way of life was based on this concept of the primacy of the aesthetic. From the design of the company letterhead, to its product line, to its factory buildings and housing estates Peter Behrens exercised his aesthetic will. He embodied the new artist who created the modern, industrial *Gesamtkunstwerk* (total work of art), expressed in Nietzsche's vision of culture as a "unity of artistic style in all manifestations of life."

Peter Behrens's success in uniting art and philosophy in a stylistic synthesis balanced the influence of Riehl. There was a certain "logical" connection between the Riehl House and Peter Behrens, for Mies's first patron played a significant role in those art circles which popularized Nietzsche as the philosopher of culture after 1900. In 1897, with *Friedrich Nietzsche als Künstler und Denker* (Friedrich Nietzsche as Artist and Thinker) Riehl was first to publish a book on Nietzsche in Germany, thereby initiating the Nietzsche cult and furthering his image at the turn of the century. In *Einführung in die Philosophie der Gegenwart* (Introduction to Contemporary Philosophy) of 1903 (Mies owned a 1908 edition) Alois Riehl again outlined Nietzsche's philosophical aesthetic, honoring him as the philosopher whose world view was the "mirror of the modern soul."

Through Riehl and Behrens Mies intimately confronted the intellectual problems of the times, keenly aware of the existential dilemma of modern man, freed from the old bonds of belief only to find his inner self in a new mental order. By his own assessment Mies began his "conscious professional career" around 1910. This consciousness awakened at a time of transition marked by many divergent theories and beginnings which appeared "confused" to Mies. His encounter with the work of Frank Lloyd Wright (first introduced to Berlin in 1910), and even more important the thoughts of the Dutch architect Hendrikus Petrus Berlage (whom Mies met in 1912 while engaged on the house project for the art collector Helene Kröller of The Hague), showed him the full spectrum of modern concepts: form, space and construction.

Behrens, Wright and Berlage interpreted these three elements of architecture very differently. Berlage's concept of the objective idea, where simple and honest construction served as the fundamental basis of all building, offered Mies, still in search of absolute values, the foundation for his "Elementarismus," which after 1919 Mies placed under the primacy of construction. With the collapse of the old order in the First World War, the renewal of *Baukunst* [8] began at a point in opposition to all accepted concepts and ideologies. Because they alone were objective, material and construction must serve as the foundation on which a new architecture would rise. Mies's Fundamentalism effectively distanced itself from all other theories and formal concepts. The house cleaning of *Baukunst* began by rejecting all aesthetic and symbolic aspects; encompassing a total resistance to art. As Mies proclaimed with appropriate pathos in his first manifesto, dated 1923, "we reject all aesthetic speculation, all doctrine, all formalism." [9]

Mies drew a line between himself and all prior art. Whether classicism, expressionism, constructivism or neoplasticism, Mies uncompromisingly branded any idea which alluded to "form" or approached "style" as "formalistic." Form no longer had a right to exist. Now quite superfluous, form was placed *ad acta* and unequivocally stricken from the catalog of architectural categories. As Mies said, "We know no form, only building problems. Form is not the aim but the result of our work. Form as such does not exist." [10]

With these words Mies subordinated artistic freedom to the ascetic virtues of impartiality and objectivity.

Like a litmus paper of conscience, at every opportunity Mies held up his categorical imperative of form. What Mies hoped for he only alluded to in his closing words: "It is our task to free the act of building from aesthetic speculators and to restore building to that which it should be alone, namely building."

Or, as he added in an informative postscript to his manuscript of the text, "To return building to that which it has always been." [11]

The future and the eternal, as these interchangeable lines imply, would rise together in the view Mies championed. A timeless, absolute law of creation would totally subjugate the new builder. It reads "*Baukunst* is the will of an epoch translated into space; living, changing, new. Not yesterday, not tomorrow, only today can be given form. Only this kind of building is creative. Create form out of the nature of the tasks with the methods of our times. This is our task." [12]

Mies hoped to conquer reality and honesty with his unconditional surrender to the myth of building and the will of the epoch. Here lay the path out of the conflict bogged down with prewar notions. With a set of projects originating between 1921 and 1924 Mies sliced through, in a single stroke, the knot of the dilemma that held *Baukunst*. The daring plans for glass skyscrapers, an office building and country houses of brick and concrete proudly departed from the time honored image of architecture, completing a radical break with historical form. Mies's creations stand alone in time, the consequence of his careful thought, fundamental conception and formal completion. Exemplary in their definition and fantastic in poetic precision, at once realistic and utopian, fully mature and complete they stand at the beginning of a new development.

These prototypes of modern architecture catapulted Mies into the first rank of the avant garde. Later as editor of *G* (for *Elementare Gestaltung*, the magazine published by Hans Richter and El Lissitzky), and as a leading member of the *Novembergruppe* Mies became one of the most important protagonists of the avant garde. His membership in the *Deutscher Werkbund* (vice president from 1926 to 1932), the *Bund Deutscher Architekten* (Union of German Architects), and the *Zehnerring* (founded 1925) indicates his concern extended beyond simply a new "art."

Mies chose to walk toward the new architecture on the path of self education in objective order. Construction and material teach the modern *Baukünstler* (building artist) whose task it is to reveal their beauty. Mies saw the secret of creating form hidden in the essence of the task, not in some historical analysis or imitation. The discipline of the new master builder began with orderly subordination to the new order of being represented by material and function. He focussed his vision on the future without sentimentality, seeing himself as the agent of the will of the epoch.

In the name of construction, material and the will of the epoch this program for a new beginning blended the Hegelian model of an objective idea with Schopenhauer's metaphysical will. From Nietzsche it inherited its hatred of academic education and of man caught in the web of historicism. Nietzsche's motto: "But the first must educate themselves," expressed Mies's thoughts in 1925 when he first announced his ideas on architectural education. In responding to the *Bund Deutscher Architekten* topic *Erziehung des baukünstlerischen Nachwuchses* (Education of the new generation of builders), Mies more or less outlined his own development when he wrote: "Everyone who has the necessary fiber should be allowed to build, regardless of origin or education. The question of educating the new generation of builders is fundamentally a question of the essence of *Baukunst*. Were this concern clearly answerable there would be no problems in education. Where the goal is fixed, the way is given. But we stand amid a transition of the hitherto fixed views. Tomorrow *Baukunst* will be thought of differently than today. Therefore, the young *Baukünstler* should not be fettered, but freed of conventions and educated in freedom of thinking and judgment. Everything else can be left to the intellectual bouts of our day. How and where that is taught is of no concern."[13]

Mies organized his architectural thoughts around the question of essence — the fundamental question to philosophy. The development of Mies's concepts is clearly legible every time he addressed the question. In his manifestoes on "*Baukunst* and the Will of the Epoch" in the early twenties or "Industrial Building" in 1924, Mies advocated an anonymous, artless building based on objectivity. Its essence manifested itself directly through materials and practical conditions, not through the invention of form based on subject. "Important and characteristic forms" emerge, Mies explained in 1924 (in a lecture using the example of Bruno Taut's plan for enlarging the city of Magdeburg), paradoxically, "just because no form was aspired to."[14]

The unexample became the example, and the new *Baukunst* stepped into an existence aptly noted by J. J. P. Oud when he wrote, "We do our work conscientiously, follow it through to the smallest detail, subordinate ourselves totally to the task, don't think of art, and, see there — one day the work is completed and shows itself to be — art."[15]

The ideas which dominated Mies's thoughts on building in 1924 appeared in a totally different light in 1927. In 1924, in "*Baukunst* and the Will of the Epoch," Mies defined the house as an effort to "organize living . . . simply from its function." Three years later he adds critical questions to his earlier assertions. In his notebook of 1927/28 he states: "The house is a commodity. May one ask for what? May one ask what the reference is? Evidently only for bodily existence. So, that all goes smoothly. And yet man has needs of the soul which cannot be satisfied with this . . . . "[16]

Early in the twenties Mies subordinated himself to the "hierarchy of things," yet by the end of the decade he added a concern for the "hierarchy of levels of knowledge."[17]

This revaluation of purpose and organization dictated a new view, yet Mies sought to escape its implications through a new definition: "Order is more than organization. Organization is setting aims. Order gives sense."[18]

This change in position, from the materialistic-positivistic "what" to the idealistic "how," occurred in 1925/26. The contradictions between his proclaimed theory and architectural projects had already hinted at the new orientation. Mies prescribed the radical therapy for *Baukunst* of self restraint in favor of objectivism which should have brought forth schematic sketches, instead Mies prepared a potion of large format perspectives which served as an aesthetic overdose. For all his awe of engineering and construction his most extraordinary aspirations are unmistakably artistic.

Closer observation of these projects shows many symbolic relics in the form of allusions to classicism. For example, in his Concrete Office Building Mies divided the end bays into three creating a structure which appears "formless" from the outside, but presents a classical A-B-A rhythm inside. Visible traces of the academic tradition also appear in the entrance done in the manner of an enclosed portal niche with pier support and expansive stairs, appearing to follow a classical solution and reminding the initiated of Schinkel's Berlin Altes Museum. Also, hardly seen at first glance, the floors gradually project out on each higher level through the progressive enlarging of the corner windows on each story. Already in 1919 J. J. P. Oud referred to the sculptural possibility concrete construction allowed in a building not only in the traditional stepping "back from bottom to top," but also the reverse, "to project *out* from bottom to top."[19]

This solution showed the functional value of the classicism Mies learned from Behrens. This hidden classicism permitted Mies the artist to do what his dogmatic theory of "building" forbade. Thus the plastic qualities of concrete, which fascinated the artist, could be honestly expressed as an aesthetic device without jeopardizing the engineering characteristic of its programmatic logic or its objectiveness.

Reducing the problem of a building to essentials did not lead to aesthetic solutions as Mies had argued. The "schematic" which existed already in the task "and therefore found expression in its character"[20] demanded suppression of the aesthetic. What the manifestoes did not mention the depicted architecture proclaimed. Mies sought to reconcile the objective world of facts and reality with his world of observed understanding. Mies the artist permitted the eyes certain rights even in his first explanation of his glass skyscrapers. Their independent shape did not result from needs of construction but depended solely on aesthetic considerations. Issues of appearance determined the surface of the skin and bone structures. He countered "the dangers of appearing dead" with the play of reflections. [21]

These architectural plans displayed qualities which Mies's theories neither allowed nor explained. Not until 1924 to 1926 did explanations appear which simultaneously permitted relaxation of this position and its reassessment after being stretched in two directions. In 1927 setting parameters became the dominant theme of Mies's position. The demands he now placed on himself and his time are marked by "lifting the tasks out of a one-sided and doctrinaire atmosphere"[22] and a "justice to both parts,"[23] that is, the objective and the subjective.

Mies set the tone for his new view in the foreword for the publication of the 1927 Weissenhofsiedlung beginning, "It is not totally meaningless today to point out that the problem of the new house is primarily a *Baukünstlerisches* artistic architectural problem, in spite of its technical and economic aspects. It is a complex problem and can be solved only through creative energy, not through calculation and organizational means."[24]

In 1924 Mies argued vehemently for a fundamental reorganization of

Ludwig Mies van der Rohe, Concrete Office Building Project. 1922. Courtesy of Museum of Modern Art.

Karl Friedrich Schinkel, Altes Museum, Berlin. 1823–30. Entrance. Courtesy of Fritz Neumeyer.

architecture through industrialization which would answer social, economic and artistic questions,[25] now, in 1927, he criticized the "clamor for 'rationalization and standardization'" which accompanied the "call for economically efficient housing," in his Weissenhof position statement.[26] Rationalization and standardization, the backbone of industrialized architecture, now appeared to be only "slogans," which did not

Ludwig Mies van der Rohe, Weissenhofsiedlung, Stuttgart. 1927. Courtesy of Fritz Neumeyer.

aim at the crux, but only aspects, of the problem. With these words Mies abandoned his position of 1924 supporting the industrialization of architecture.

The change in Mies's position between 1924 and 1927 is marked by his moving from materialism toward idealism. This change is reflected in his statement of 1924 when Mies saw the "central problem of architecture today" as one of "a question of materials" and 1927 when he considered it "basically an intellectual problem."[27] For Mies the "creative energies" of the intellect won out over calculating and organizational means.

At the 1930 convention of the *Deutscher Werkbund* in Vienna, Mies concluded his speech by reaffirming his new position and by denying mechanistic and functionalistic doctrine, a doctrine he would later equate with modern architecture. He said,

The new era is a fact: it exists, irrespective of our 'yes' or 'no.' It is pure fact . . . .
One thing will be decisive: how we will assert ourselves in the face of facts. Here the problems of the spirit begin. Not the 'what' but alone the 'how' is decisive. That we produce goods and with what means we fabricate is of no intellectual consequence.
Whether we build high or low, with steel or glass, says nothing about the value of these structures.
Whether we strive for centralization or decentralization in our cities is a practical question, not one of value.
Yet it is the question of value which is decisive.
We must set new values, note ultimate function, to establish new measures.
Sense and justice of any era, also the new one, lies singularly and alone in the supposition that the spirit is given the right to exist.[28]

These sentences speak in terms of closeness and distance, calling and warning, yes and no. Perceived as one of the outstanding figures of modern architecture because of the Barcelona Pavilion and Tugendhat House, Mies accepted the objectiveness of the epoch as a necessary fact — which no doubt held its own possibilities — but denied it as a goal and theme of *Baukunst*. In opening his campaign on two fronts, Mies countered any type of one sidedness, allowing neither the objective power of technology, nor the individual act of free interpretation by an artist-individual to be given preference.

For Mies the architect's decisive consideration was not principally practical but philosophical. One built not so much to provide functional living space, but to define a specific quality of life. The concept of quality was not a retreat into elitism, but a stride toward an optimal solution

achieving results on a broad scale. Mies founded this conviction on his view of the social function of art and *Baukunst*. When called to the Bauhaus in 1930 Mies incorporated this notion into his principles of teaching thereby giving the Bauhaus a new structure. In his 1928 lecture *Die Voraussetzungen baukünstlerischen Schaffens* (The Prerequisites for Creating Artistic Construction), Mies proposed that teaching offered the possibility "of unfolding consciously artistic and spiritual values in the hard and clear atmosphere of technology."[29]

In striving toward this intellectual goal Mies saw himself allied with the philosopher of religion Romano Guardini and the architect Rudolf Schwarz, both of whom he knew. As late as 1950 Mies based his philosophy of *Baukunst* on their concepts of *baukünstlerischer Erziehung* (learning artistic construction), concepts Mies had formulated in 1938. With the transformation of two decades of self discovery into an uncomplicated, unified mental construct, Mies said goodbye to Europe. His acceptance speech for the position of Director of the School of Architecture at the Armour Institute of Technology in 1938, composed in Germany before his departure, marks the end of his European career. Nowhere else does Mies express his philosophy of *Baukunst* with such logic, clarity, perception and conviction. While all around him architectural culture was borne to the grave by the rhythm of marching feet, Mies created in a few pages a concept of an ideal order in which "the world of our creation should begin to flower anew."[30]

The Miesian order of *Baukunst*, following the method of architectural education Mies had learned through the philosophical writings of Romano Guardini, Georg Simmel, Max Scheler, Eduard Spranger and Henri Bergson derived from a philosophy of opposites and its effect on culture. From this philosophy Mies unfolded his own order of opposites which leads to a higher unity. For Mies the primary differentiation lay between man's "vital existence" and value, founded in man's "spiritual designation" and made possible by his "spiritual being." Mies's point of departure was set: "Our definition of purpose defines the character of our civilization, our definition of value the light of our culture." Therefore "genuine learning" aimed "not only at purpose but also at value."[31] From this totality of opposites the premise of *Baukunst* is derived: "As much as purpose and value are essentially opposites and from different levels, they are united. What else should our value system make reference to if not value. Both realms together predicate human existence . . . If these notions are true for all human endeavor, even for the slightest hint of value, how much more binding must they be in the realm of *Baukunst*. The essence of *Baukunst* is rooted totally in the purposeful. But it reaches across all levels of value, to the realm of spiritual being, into the realm of reason, the sphere of pure art. Every method of architectural education must account for this fact . . . . "

For Mies building followed a route of realization, which made "clear" step by step " . . . that which is possible, necessary and sensible," in order to get "from the irresponsibility of opinion to the responsibility of insight," and thereby achieve "the clear conformity of spiritual order." Again the stations the architect passed in order to find himself and his way to *Baukunst* are autobiographical: "The disciplined path from material through purposes of building" to "the sphere of pure art," duplicates the route Mies took from an apprenticeship as a stone mason through his radical material and functional concerns of the early twenties to the final idealistic creation of 1929.

The scope of the above dimensions becomes clear through comparison of the following assertions. In 1938 Mies led his listeners, just as in his 1923 lecture *Solved Problems* into the "healthy world of primitive building." In 1923 Mies asked his audience, "Have you ever seen anything more complete in fulfilling its function and in its use of material?" while showing them a leaf hut and other primitive skin and bone structures created out of walrus ribs and seal hides.[32] But in 1938, these marvels had broader implications, for aesthetic interest added to these basic creations where "every ax bite still had meaning and where a chisel mark was a genuine exclamation." Mies continued, "What feeling for material and what power of expression speaks in these buildings? What warmth they radiate, and how beautiful they are. They echo like old songs. In stone structures we find the same. Which natural urge does it express? . . . Where do we find such a wealth in structure. Where else but here do we find a healthier strength and natural beauty. With what self assured clarity does the beamed ceiling rest on this old masonry and with what feeling was a door cut out of these walls."

The "unknown master" who created these elemental images of existence had a clear and natural understanding of materials, imbuing them with symbolic meaning. The building of any epoch could be an example. Here opposing realms of life, vital existence and spiritual being, created an almost self-evident and therefore generally acceptable unity. A similar bridge between subject and object, carrying the concept of culture as a single unit, exists for contemporary man when

Pygmy Village. c.1905. Courtesy of James J. Harrison, *Life Among the Pygmies*, 1905.

exercising authority over modern materials and techniques. But he had not yet dared to build. The existence of these means in themselves does not presuppose a value. Therefore, as Mies points out, there need exist no modern feelings of superiority over primitive building: "We promise ourselves nothing from the materials, but only their proper handling. Even the new materials do not assure us superiority. Each material is only worth that which we make out of it."[33]

Only an understanding of those possibilities hidden in the essence of a material leads to a fundamental understanding of real form. The questions must be asked: "We want to know what it can be, what it must be, and what it may not be. We want to know its essence."

Aside from the nature of materials and the nature of function, *Baukunst* demands to know "the spiritual place in which we are," and to discern the "sustaining and driving forces." Only after this is known can a critic of the epoch be possible: "We will attempt to pose real questions. Questions of value and of the purpose of technology. We want to show that it [technology] lends us not only might and grandeur but also contains risks. That technology too, is subject to good and evil. And that man must make the right decision."

Yet every decision — and here Mies pursues the logical construction of his spiritual home without limit — leads to a specific order: "Therefore we want to illuminate the possible orders and clarify their principles." The fundamental division into materialistic and idealistic order with which Mies finally concludes brings his philosophical experiences and architectural possibilities to their lowest common denominator. Mies says, "the mechanical principle of order," with which the buildings of 1923 were branded through an "overemphasis of material and functional tendencies," were rejected because they did not satisfy "our sense of the servile function of material and our interest in integrity and value." The "idealistic principle of order" to which his ideal buildings of 1929/31 related also could not be affirmed, because in its "overemphasis of the ideal and formal" it neither satisfied interest in "truth and simplicity" nor "practical reason."

Mies made no decision for his "organic principle of order," aimed at a "sense and purpose of measure of the parts." This principle, not to be interpreted in the sense of a biological parallel, derived its intellectual and conceptual counterpart from Romano Guardini's *Philosophie des Lebendig-Konkreten*, which recalled Plato *and* Nietzsche. For Guardini organic designated that sphere of life in which the contradictions of matter and spirit, purpose and value, technique and art might possibly refer to a mutually inclusive existence. In it lay hidden the creative principle which could bring man and things together, which through the "proportions between things"[34] brought forth beauty.

Mies concluded his 1938 address with St. Augustine. Already in 1928 Mies saw in him a brilliant founder of order who sought to introduce a spiritual measure into life by aiming at "one goal," namely that of "creating order in the desperate confusion of our time," to transform chaos to cosmos. Mies concluded, "But we want an order which allows each thing its place. And we want to give each thing its due according to its nature. That we want to do so completely that the world of our creations begins to blossom from within. More we do not want. More we cannot do. Through nothing the sense and goal of our work is made more manifest than the profound words of St. Augustine: 'Beauty is the splendor of truth'."

This "Summa Theologica" of Miesian *Baukunst* was binding. As the 1965 publication, *Thoughts on the education in Baukunst* indicated nothing new could be added. The principle framework of Mies's *Baukunst*, as outlined in his 1938 lecture, was set and final.

Only by passing through an objective order could man attain a "self worth, which is called his culture." Out of this "the object becomes the subject and the subject becomes the object," (after a concept expressed by Georg Simmel in his essay, "Philosophy of Culture," which Mies owned), the specific, which defined the cultural process, is created.[35] In an analogous context Mies saw technology as "a genuine cultural movement . . . a world unto itself." From the encounter of technology and *Baukunst* architecture emerged in the sense of the "culture of building." Mies said, "It is our sincere hope that they will unite, that some day one will be the expression of the other. Only then will we have architecture as the true symbol of the epoch."[36]

The treadmill of history, the eternal return of the metaphysical bridgehead, which marked Simmel's Nietzsche inspired concept of

Ludwig Mies van der Rohe standing before the steel skeleton of the Farnsworth House, Plano. c.1950. Courtesy of Fritz Neumeyer.

culture, found expression in Mies, who said, "In endlessly slow gestation the grand form is created whose birthing is the function of the epoch . . . Not all that occurs, is carried out in the realm of the visible. The decisive engagements of the intellect are decided on invisible battlefields. The visible is only the last step of an historic fact. Its realization. Its true realization. Then it ends. And a new world arises."[37]

The steel skeleton embodied and symbolized for Mies that objective order through which the *Baukunst* of the age steps toward educational self-recognition and technical order which may then be transformed into culture. Mies strove to lay the foundation for such an objective culture, in which technical and spiritual values merged to form a higher unity and rise in "self-realization" (Simmel). His concept of *Baukunst* sought to integrate the new world of construction into the humanistic cosmos. It is "simultaneously radical and conservative, radical, because it affirms the scholarly power to carry and drive our age . . . conservative, because it not only serves a purpose, but also a value, and it is subject not only to function, but also expression. It is conservative because it is founded on the eternal truths of architecture: order, space, proportion."[38]

The "disciplined path" from material through purpose to idea is the *curriculum vitae* which Mies followed in his own self-education. It did not trust in the teachability of *Baukunst* but in the training of hand, eye and mind. It is in this sense that Mies's words, "fulfill the law to win freedom"[39] are meant. [Translated by Rolf Achilles]

NOTES

1 Katherine Kuh, "Mies van der Rohe: Modern Classicist," *Saturday Review*, 23 January 1965, p.61.

2 Adolf Loos, *Trotzdem 1900–1930*, Innsbruck, 1931, p.101.

3 Franz Schulze, *Mies van der Rohe: A Critical Biography*, Chicago: University of Chicago Press, 1985, pp.17–18.

4 Doris Schmidt, "Gläserne Wände für den Blick auf die Welt — Zum Tode Mies van der Rohe," *Süddeutsche Zeitung*, Nr.198, 19 August 1969, p.11, quoted from Wolfgang Frieg, *Ludwig Mies van der Rohe: Das europäische Werk 1907–1937*, Bonn, 1976, (Diss.), p. 60.

5 On Mies's notebook and his relation to philosophy see my book: *Mies van der Rohe – Das kunstlose Wort. Gedanken zur Baukunst*, Berlin, 1986.

6 Mies in conversation with Peter Carter, *Bauen und Wohnen*, 16, 1961, p. 230 ff.

7 Rudolf Fahrner, ed., *Paul Thiersch, Leben und Werk*, Berlin, 1970, p. 27. Also, in conversation with Dirk Lohan, Mies said, "When I had completed the house (Riehl), Thiersch, whom we recently heard from, came. Thiersch had been with Behrens, and then became office supervisor for Bruno Paul, and he said to me that Behrens had asked him to tell him when he had some good people and to send these people to him. He told me, 'You should really go see him, he's a top man.' That's how I came to Behrens." Unpublished manuscript, Mies Archive, Museum of Modern Art, [MoMA].

8 [Translator's note: the term *Baukunst* is not translated in this essay. It is an important concept for Mies and has been variously translated as the art of building, the art of construction, and building art.]

9 Mies van der Rohe, "Arbeitsthesen," G, nr. 1, July 1923, p. 3.

10 Mies van der Rohe, "Bauen," G, nr. 2, September 1923, p. 1. ff.

11 Note on the verso of the manuscript "Betonhaus," 1 October 1923, Mies Archive, Library of Congress, [LC].

12 Mies van der Rohe, "Bauen," G, nr. 2, September 1923, p. 1.

13 Mies van der Rohe, letter to the BDA-Berlin, 16 June 1925, Mies Archive, MoMA.

14 Mies van der Rohe, Lecture Manuscript, 19 June 1924. Dirk Lohan Archive.

15 J. J. P. Oud, "Wohin führt das neue Bauen: Kunst und Standard," *Die Form*, 3, 1928, p. 61.

16 Mies's notebook, fol. 22, Mies Archive, MoMA.

17 Mies van der Rohe, Lecture Manuscript on art criticism, 1930, fol. 5, Mies Archive, MoMA.

18 Mies van der Rohe, Lecture Manuscript, Chicago, undated, (c. 1960), Mies Archive, LC.

19 J. J. P. Oud, "Über die zukünftige Baukunst und ihre architektonischen Möglichkeiten," *Frühlicht* 1, 1922, Heft 4. Reprinted in Bruno Taut, *Frühlicht 1920–1922*, Berlin, 1963, p. 206. Mies's first essay "Hochhäuser," also appeared in this magazine.

20 See note 14.

21 Mies van der Rohe, "Hochhäuser."

22 Mies van der Rohe, ["Foreword,"] *Bau und Wohnung*, Stuttgart: Deutscher Werkbund, 1927, p. 7.

23 Mies van der Rohe, "Zu meinem Block," *Bau und Wohnung*.

24 See note 22.

25 Mies van der Rohe, "Industrielles Bauen," G, Nr. 3, June 1924, p. 8ff.

26 Mies van der Rohe, "Preliminary comments to the first special publication of the Werkbund-exhibit," *Die Wohnung*, Stuttgart, 1927, in *Die Form*, 2, 1927, H. 9, p. 257.

27 *ibid.*

28 Mies van der Rohe, "Die neu Zeit," *Die Form*, 5, 1930, H. 15, p. 406.

29 Mies van der Rohe, "Die Voraussetzungen baukünstlerischen Schaffens," Lecture, February, 1928, Dirk Lohan Archive.

30 Mies van der Rohe, [Inaugural Address as Director of Architecture at Armour Institute of Technology,] presented at the Testimonial Dinner in the Palmer House, Chicago, 18 October 1938.

31 Various Mies quotes with no special context. On the differentiation of value and purpose Mies marked several passages in Alois Riehl, *Zur Einführung in die Philosophie der Gegenwart*, Leipzig, 1908, especially p. 9, p. 183f. (double markings) and p. 187f. (double markings along passage on values, beliefs, morals and production). Copy in Dirk Lohan Archive.

32 See Appendix for complete text of Mies's 1923 lecture.

33 Mies marked passages in Eduard Spranger, *Lebensformen. Geisteswissenschaftliche Psychologie und Ethik der Persönlichkeit*, Halle/Salle, 1922, p. 325f., on the question of life and technology.

34 Excerpted from an interview with the *Bayrischer Rundfunk* (Bavarian Radio) on the occasion of Mies's 80th birthday; published in *Der Architekt*, 15, 1966, H. 10. p. 324, where Mies discusses *Baukunst*. See also, Mies van der Rohe, "Schön und praktisch bauen! Schluss mit der kalten Zweckmäszigkeit," *Duisburger Generalanzeiger*, 49, 26 January 1930, p. 2, where Mies discusses beauty. Also, Mies van der Rohe, Radio Address Manuscript, 17 August 1931, Dirk Lohan Archive, where Mies discusses proportion.

35 Georg Simmel, "Zur Philosophie der Kultur. Der Begriff und die Tragödie der Kultur," in Georg Simmel, *Philosophische Kultur. Gesammelte Essais*, Leipzig, 1911, p. 203. Copy in Dirk Lohan Archive.

36 Mies van der Rohe, "Architecture and Technology," *Arts and Architecture*, 67, 1950, vol. 10. p. 30.

37 Mies van der Rohe, Lecture, Chicago, (c.1950), Mies Archive, LC, fol. 17, 18.

38 Mies van der Rohe, quoted by Peter Carter, *Bauen und Wohnen*, 16, 1961, p. 239.

39 See note 37.

MIES VAN DER ROHE: ARCHITECT AND TEACHER IN GERMANY

Sandra Honey

True education is concerned not only with practical goals but also with values. By practical aims we are bound to the specific structure of our epoch. Our values, on the other hand, are rooted in the spiritual nature of men.

If teaching has any purpose, it is to implant true insight and responsibility. Education must lead us from irresponsible opinion to true responsibility.
It must lead us from chance and arbitrariness to rational clarity and order.

The long path from material through function to creative work has only a single goal: to create order out of the desperate confusion of our time.[1]

When he addressed the Armour Institute of Technology in 1938, Mies van der Rohe, uprooted from his native Germany at the age of fifty-two, struggled to convey his principles to an audience which knew little of his culture, or the struggles of his generation — the architects who, in two decades, had created European modern architecture.

In this speech Mies presented the core of his teaching, the relation of architecture to its period and the expression of the period's sustaining force. Among his generation, Mies sought to interpret the spirit of the time in his architecture. He demonstrated how to translate theory into an architecture of simplicity and beauty. His genius lies in this intense clarity of perception.

Mies ended his inaugural speech by saying "Nothing can express the aim and meaning of our work better than the profound words of St. Augustine: 'Beauty is the splendor of Truth'."[2]

On this high moral note he began a long teaching career in Chicago. If his teaching is to be fully appreciated and his educational principles are to guide the student towards the goals Mies set for himself, an understanding of his methods is essential, for he said, "We must understand the motives and forces of our time and analyze their structure from three points of view: the material, the functional and the spiritual."[3]

Some of the motives and forces inspiring Mies's generation were expressed in pamphlets and manifestos published by such organizations as the *Deutscher Werkbund* and the Bauhaus. Many architects were obsessed with the birth of the new technological society and the form this society would generate.

More than any other architect of his generation, Mies penetrated the discussion and isolated its significant aspects and ideas. He defended the art of architecture and once, in an impromptu speech, he explained,

The role of the critic is to test a work of art from the point of view of significance and value. To do this, however, the critic must first understand the work of art. This is not easy. Works of art have a life of their own; they are not accessible to everyone. If they are to have meaning for us we must approach them on their own terms.[4]

Mies left his native Aachen in 1905 and moved to Berlin, where within three months he apprenticed to Bruno Paul, a Bavarian, who headed the School of the Decorative Arts Museum where Mies registered for two years.

Mies left Paul on receiving his first architectural commission — the Riehl house near Potsdam. Professor Riehl sent Mies to Italy for three months and on his return he designed a simple house in the local manner. In 1908 Mies joined the office of Peter Behrens who was then chief designer and architect for A.E.G., the German electrical company. Behrens, the most influential architect in Berlin, had been a leading exponent of the Art Nouveau Movement brought to Germany by Henri

Ludwig Mies van der Rohe, Riehl House, Berlin-Neubabelsberg. 1907. Courtesy of Bertel Thorn Prikker.

van de Velde. Hermann Muthesius, a close friend and collaborator of Behrens, reported on the English Arts and Crafts Movement on his return to Berlin in 1903. Muthesius interpreted the planning of the English country house as functional and declared that scientific *Sachlichkeit* (objectivity) was to guide architecture. He insisted that architecture and design should merge into a single discipline becoming a *Gesamtkunstwerk* where every article of daily use and the structures of engineers should belong to the field and activity of the architect-designer.

Although Muthesius was not a founding member of the *Werkbund*, he was the first to formulate what later would become part of its program. Muthesius said the *Werkbund* should "help form recover its rights," and be the creator and perpetrator of a German taste industry, aided by state policy. Mies said of his stay in Behrens's office that, "It then became clear to me that it was not the task of architecture to invent form. I tried to understand what that task was. I asked Peter Behrens, but he could not give me an answer."[5]

Mies supervised construction of Behrens's embassy building in St. Petersburg — a monumental edifice modeled on Schinkel's Altes Museum. While working for Behrens, Mies was commissioned privately to build the Villa Perls in 1911. The smooth, symmetrical elevations of this simple neo-classical villa resemble Behrens's stripped classical work of the same period.

Mies recalled that, "Under Behrens I learnt the grand form, if you see what I mean, the monumental."[6]

Also at this time Mies studied Schinkel, especially his scale, proportion and rhythm. In 1912 Mies traveled to The Hague with Behrens's scheme for the Kröller-Müller family house, and he stayed when he gained the commission himself, but which he never completed. He now studied Berlage who, Mies said, "was a man of great seriousness who would not accept anything that was fake and it was he who had said that nothing should be built that is not clearly constructed."[7]

Berlage despised the irrelevant, preaching the elementary truths of the primacy of space, the importance of walls as creators of form, and the need for systematic proportion. He declared that, "Before all else the wall must be shown in all its sleek beauty. Its nature as a plane must remain."

Through his stay in Holland, Mies rediscovered the brick. The influence of Schinkel and Berlage remained with Mies throughout his career.

Ludwig Mies van der Rohe, Perls House, Berlin-Zehlendorf. 1911. Courtesy of Bertel Thorn Prikker.

The development of the new rational German architecture was slowed by four years of war. By 1919 utopian idealism and exuberant individualism in nearly every German city led artists, architects and sculptors to found revolutionary societies to bring modern art to the people. Berlin became the most active center of art and culture in Europe in the early 1920's. It sucked in such new movements as Dutch De Stijl, Russian Constructivism and Suprematism, Swiss Dadaism, and French Cubism and Purism, and the pre-war German Expressionist Movement regained momentum. New radical periodicals proliferated; established magazines became radical, while editorial policies varied, they all claimed modern art alone could bring culture to the people. They all demanded state patronage.

Ludwig Mies van der Rohe, Kröller House Project, The Hague. 1911. Full scale model. Courtesy of Museum of Modern Art.

Ludwig Mies van der Rohe, Glass
Skyscraper Project, Friedrichstrasse,
Berlin. 1921. First scheme. Collage.
Courtesy of Edward A. Duckett.

Through *Glass Architecture*, published in 1914, Paul Scheerbart, the poet of crystal architecture inspired Bruno Taut's Glass Chain Circle. Taut's "Architektur-Programm" of 1918 laid down the aims and ideals later adopted by the organizers of the great German social housing program, and it also inspired Gropius's program for the Bauhaus.

For his project in the Friedrichstrasse Competition of January 1922, Mies proposed an all glass office building on a prismatic plan to fit the triangular site. Later in 1922 he drew another glass skyscraper, on a faceted, free-form, curvilinear plan, for an imaginary site. These projects were illustrated in *Frühlicht* in 1922, to which Mies wrote,

Skyscrapers reveal their bold structural pattern during construction. Only then does the gigantic steel web seem impressive. When the outer walls are put in place, the structural system which is the basis of all artistic design, is hidden by a chaos of meaningless and trivial forms. When finished, these buildings are impressive only because of their size; yet they could surely be more than mere examples of our technical ability. Instead of trying to solve the new problems with old forms, we should develop the new forms from the very nature of the new problems.[8]

Mies began to understand glass in the rational terms of the new order. This approach to architecture by Mies and others came to be known as *sachlich* or *sweck* architecture, and the term *Die neue Sachlichkeit* (the new objectivity or practicality) was used to describe the movement. During 1923 the ideas of Le Corbusier, the Constructivists and the De Stijl Group began to exert a strong influence in Germany. The De Stijl collaborators defined the form of the new architecture. Van Doesburg's manifesto, "Towards a Plastic Architecture," published in 1924, proclaimed the new architecture was elemental, economic, functional, formal, open, anti-cubic, asymmetrical, non-repetitious, and knew no basic type. From these proclamations the De Stijl architects, drawing on Berlage and Wright, arrived at a simple formula of plain vertical walls and flat roofs, free of decorative elements.

Van Doesburg settled in Weimar from 1921 to 1923 to be close to the Bauhaus, founded in 1919 by Walter Gropius. Here he held a design course for Bauhaus and other interested students, organized a congress of Constructivists and Dadaists, and lectured extensively. Van Doesburg encouraged the Bauhaus to change its outlook, although László Moholy-Nagy, the Hungarian Constructivist, had more effect in the matter. He took over the *Vorkurs* from Johannes Itten. Romanticism, mysticism and medievalism lost ground.

In 1923, after four years of activity the Bauhaus published a curriculum which most students followed loosely. The Bauhaus slogan changed from "Art and Handicrafts" to "Art and Technology — A New Unity." At his atelier in Berlin, Mies was an excellent host. He shared his work space with Hugo Häring, and they kept up a constant dialogue. Mies gave insight into his discussions with Häring and others when he wrote in 1924 that,

Greek temples, Roman basilicas and medieval cathedrals are significant to us as creations of a whole epoch rather than as works of individual architects.... Such buildings are impersonal by nature. They are pure expressions of their time. Their true meaning is that they are symbols of their epoch.
Architecture is the will of the epoch translated into space. Until this simple truth is clearly recognized, the new architecture will be uncertain and tentative. Until then it must remain a chaos of undirected forces. The question as to the nature of architecture is of decisive importance. It must be understood that all architecture is bound up with its own time, that it can only be manifested in living tasks and in the medium of its epoch. In no age has it been otherwise.
The demand of our time for realism and functionalism must be met. Only then will our buildings express the potential greatness of our time....
Our utilitarian buildings can become worthy of the name of architecture only if they truly interpret their time by their perfect functional expression.[9]

Mies joined the *Novembergruppe* in late 1921, becoming chairman of the organizing committee for architectural exhibits, a position he held until 1926.

During 1923 and 1924 some of the architects in the *Novembergruppe* gathered in Mies's office to discuss developments. Among them were Otto Bartning, Walter Curt Behrendt, Ludwig Hilberseimer, Hans Poelzig, Bruno and Max Taut, Häring and Mies, and they became known as the *Zehner Ring* (Circle of Ten). Later, the circle expanded to include Behrens, Gropius, the Luckhardt brothers, Ernst May, Hans Scharoun and Martin Wagner. For its duration, it remained a loose, informal association, without a constitution or a head.

The *G Group* also drew membership from the *Novembergruppe*, including six De Stijl collaborators, the Constructivist El Lissitsky, Mies, Hilberseimer and Friedrich Kiesler. Hans Richter and Werner Graeff organized the publication of *Zeitschrift für Elementare Gestaltung*, known as *G*, with themselves and Lissitsky as editors. Mies replaced Lissitsky on the editorial board of *G 2*, September 1923, and he financed the publication of *G 3* which appeared in June 1924 in a new format. The fourth and final issue of *G* appeared in March 1926.

G 1 produced slogans and ideas, varied in origin, but with a constant theme of elemental creativity brought to the magazine by El Lissitsky. It included Mies's Concrete Office Building Project of 1923 of which Mies wrote,

The office building is a house of work, of organization, of clarity, of economy. Broad, light workspace, unbroken, but articulated according to the organization of the work. Maximum effect with minimum means.
The materials: concrete, steel, glass.
Reinforced concrete structures are skeletons by nature. No trimmings. No fortress. Columns and girders eliminate load-bearing walls. This is skin and bone construction.[10]

In the same issue, speaking for the *G Group*, Mies declared,

We reject all aesthetic speculation, all doctrine, all formalism.
Architecture is the will of an epoch translated into space; living, changing, new.
Not yesterday, not tomorrow, only today can be given form.
Only this kind of building will be creative.
Create form out of the nature of our tasks with the methods of our time.
This is our task.

The Concrete Office Building can now be traced in part to Schinkel's Altes Museum, and Mies said later that he was "a little inspired by the Palazzo Pitti, for I wanted to see if we could make something of similar strength with our means, and for our purposes."[11]
G 2 concentrated on executed works and projects of group members. It included a photograph of the model of Mies's Concrete Country House project of 1923, and his anti-formalist manifesto:

We refuse to recognize problems of form, but only problems of building.
Form is not the aim of our work, but only the result.
Form, by itself, does not exist.
Form as an aim is formalism; and that we reject.
Essentially our task is to free the practice of building from the control of aesthetic speculators and restore it to what it should exclusively be: building.

All *G Group* statements took a hard uncompromising position.
G 3 appeared in June 1924 with Mies's 1922 glass skyscraper project on the cover, and a montaged drawing of his Friedrichstrasse Competition project illustrated Richter's editorial. In this issue Mies wrote,

Industrialization of the processes of construction is a question of materials. Our first consideration, therefore, must be to find a new building material. Our technologists must and will succeed in inventing a material which can be industrially manufactured and processed and which will be weatherproof, soundproof and insulating. It must be a light material which not only permits but

Ludwig Mies van der Rohe, Concrete Office Building Project. 1922. Drawing. Courtesy of Museum of Modern Art.

requires industrial production. All the parts will be made in a factory and the work at the site will consist only of assemblage, requiring extremely few man-hours. This will greatly reduce building costs. Then the new architecture will come into its own.[12]

Although slow to declare his modern ideas, from 1923 on Mies played a major role. For reasons not yet clear leadership of the Ring fell to Mies, and his authority increased as the years passed.
From 1919 to 1923 Germany experienced great social unrest and political turmoil. From 1925 to 1930 building increased considerably through mass housing developments financed by various federal, state,

Ludwig Mies van der Rohe, Concrete Country House Project. 1924. Model. Courtesy of Museum of Modern Art.

Ludwig Mies van der Rohe, Municipal
Housing Development,
Afrikanischestrasse, Berlin. 1925.
Courtesy of Museum of Modern Art.

Ludwig Mies van der Rohe,
Weissenhofsiedlung, Stuttgart. 1924.
Model of first scheme. Courtesy of Fritz
Neumeyer.

municipal political and commercial agencies. Inspiration for these housing programs came primarily from Bruno Taut. His concern was no less than the restructuring of society.

In 1924, architects of the new housing took a different approach: the new dwelling had to be reorganized and more advanced technology used to alleviate space problems within cities. The first real progress was made in Frankfurt, where Ernst May was appointed City Architect in 1925, and construction began on housing estates built to the most stringent budgets. At the same time, Martin Wagner was appointed to the same post in Berlin. The impetus for the new style of housing came from building societies, particularly from the largest of them, GEHAG, which at Wagner's request appointed Taut as chief designer.

Mies's contribution to social housing in Berlin was a relatively small development on Afrikanische Strasse (1926–27), three slab blocks and an end block with some communal facilities. Among the most distinguished of such developments, Mies's buildings were well planned, relatively spacious, with well proportioned elevations.

Widespread publicity for the new German architecture came in 1927 from an experimental housing project, the Weissenhof Exhibition, organized by Mies and the *Deutscher Werkbund*. In 1925 the *Werkbund* began to publish *Die Form*, a magazine of attractive and lavish format. It addressed every aspect of architecture and design. In 1927 Mies van der Rohe made his first contribution to the *Werkbund* discussion of form in a letter to the editor,

Dear Dr. Riezler,
I do not oppose form, but only form as an end in itself. And I do this as the result of a number of experiences and the insight I have gained from them.
Form as an end inevitably results in formalism. For the effort is directed only to the exterior. But only what has life on the inside has a living exterior.[13]

Mies's appointment as First Vice President of the *Werkbund*, responsible for its exhibition programs, coincided with the decision to stage the first major exhibition since Cologne in 1914 at Weissenhof, a suburb of Stuttgart. As director Mies controlled planning and architecture. His first scheme for the hilltop site conceived a unified community crowned by a horizontal block, in the manner of Taut's *Die Stadtkrone*. When the city insisted on freestanding units, separated by motor roads, Mies split the site into irregular plots.

By autumn 1926 Mies had chosen the architects to participate, and scheduled the exhibition to open in summer 1927. In the interests of

uniformity, he stipulated that all buildings have a flat roof and smooth white finish. In his foreword to the exhibition catalogue he wrote,

The problem of the modern dwelling is primarily architectural, in spite of its technical and economic aspects. It is a complex problem of planning and can therefore be solved only by creative minds, not by calculation or organization. Therefore, I felt it imperative, in spite of current talk about rationalization and standardization, to keep the project at Stuttgart free from being one-sided or doctrinaire. I have therefore invited leading representatives of the modern movement to make their contribution to the problem of the modern dwelling.

The foreign architects were Le Corbusier with Pierre Jeanneret (Paris), J.J.P. Oud and Mart Stam (Rotterdam), Josef Frank (Vienna), and Victor Bourgeois (Brussels). Of the German architects he selected Behrens, Poelzig, the Taut brothers, Hilberseimer, Gropius from Berlin, Rading and Scharoun from Breslau, while Döcker and Schneck represented Stuttgart. Of Berlin architects the only significant omission was Mendelsohn, for Häring was invited but declined.

The Weissenhof development attempted to explore new technical methods of construction. The buildings were far too luxurious and expensive to be prototypes for mass housing. In his block Mies demonstrated the potential of steel frame construction, with fixed stairwells and service cores, and flexible internal planning.

Walter Curt Behrendt's *Der Sieg des neuen Baustils* (The Victory of the New Building Style) portrayed the atmosphere of 1927 in Germany, and showed that the Weissenhofsiedlung demonstrated how progressive architecture, whether by Le Corbusier, De Stijl or from Berlin, had

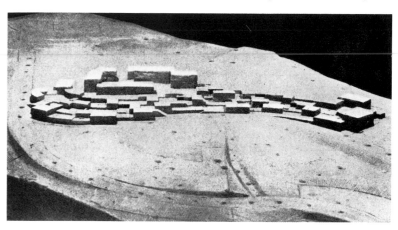

merged into a single aesthetic under the orchestration of Mies van der Rohe.

The international character of the new architecture was celebrated by critics and architects. Gropius had published *Internationale Architektur* in 1925; and in 1927 Hilberseimer published *Internationale Neue Baukunst*, followed by three other books on different aspects of the new style. Opposition also strengthened, with Alexander von Senger's *Krisis der Architektur* published in 1928 attacking modern architecture as a whole.

From 1928 a new more realistic phase of modern architecture emerged characterized by the *Congrés Internationale d'Architecture Moderne* (CIAM) and the Dutch group, *de 8*. The first CIAM meeting ended with the La Sarraz Declaration that,

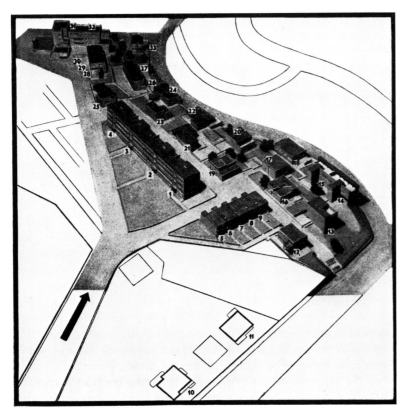

The destiny of architecture is to express the orientation of the age. Works of architecture can spring only from the present time.

Delegates from European national associations affirm today the need for a new conception in architecture that satisfies the spiritual, intellectual and material demands of present-day life. Conscious of the deep disturbances of the social structure brought about by machines, they recognize that the transformation of economic order and of social life inescapably brings with it a corresponding transformation of the architectural phenomenon.

Hannes Meyer, who replaced Gropius at the Bauhaus in 1928, published his functionalist theory in the Bauhaus Yearbook entitled "*Bauen*,"

All things in this world are a product of the formula: (function times economy).
All things are, therefore, not works of art.
All life is function and therefore unartistic.

In 1929, Bruno Taut echoed Meyer's theory, but added that beauty, a concept foreign to Meyer, would come from efficiency:

The first and foremost point at issue in any building should be how to attain the utmost utility.
If everything is founded on sound efficiency, this efficiency itself, or rather its utility, will form its own aesthetic law.
The aim of architecture is the creation of perfect and, therefore, beautiful efficiency.

While publicly and politically funded social housing kept many radical architects busy, Mies van der Rohe's wealthy patrons allowed him to consolidate his practice. He built a monument to the Communists Karl Liebknecht and Rosa Luxembourg, and the Wolf, (Guben, 1925–1926), and Lange and Esters Houses (Krefeld, 1928–30). Developed from his Concrete Country House project of 1923, Mies attempted to modernize Wright. The smooth, refined brickwork was Dutch in influence, the facades were unarticulated.

In 1928 and 1929, Mies entered four competitions: the replanning of Alexanderplatz, and the Adam Building (Berlin, 1928), a bank building (Stuttgart, 1928), and another office building on Friedrichstrasse (Berlin, 1929 — the same triangular site as the 1922 competition).

Mies continued to organize *Werkbund* exhibitions until his resignation in 1932. At the Barcelona International Exhibition in 1929, Mies designed and built the A.E.G. exhibition hall and laid out all the exhibits. Lilly Reich, Mies's colleague and frequent collaborator, had designed *Werkbund* exhibits at the Frankfurt Fair from 1924 to 1927. In 1926 she

Ludwig Mies van der Rohe, Wolf House, Guben. 1926. Courtesy of Museum of Modern Art.

Ludwig Mies van der Rohe, Hermann Lange House, Krefeld. 1928. Courtesy of Museum of Modern Art.

Ludwig Mies van der Rohe, Weissenhofsiedlung, Stuttgart. 1925. Aerial view of model, final scheme. Courtesy of Fritz Neumeyer.

moved to Berlin where she administered Mies's practice and ran her own interior design business with showrooms just down the street from Mies's office.

Lilly Reich designed Mies's exhibit at the *Mode der Dame* Exhibition, Berlin, 1927 — the Velvet and Silk Cafe. This displayed Mies's tubular steel furniture — his first furniture — for mass production. In the Tugendhat House (Brno, 1928–1930), the most stunningly luxurious house of the decade, Lilly Reich designed the interior decorations. During their collaboration (1927–1939), she added to Mies's work a luxurious richness in color and texture which remains unsurpassed.

Mies van der Rohe's German National Pavilion at Barcelona became a symbol of the decade, 1919–1929. Mies returned to the balanced, asymmetric composition of free standing walls and flowing space of the Brick Country House project of 1923, but the theoretically endless space of the earlier project was subtly controlled.

At Barcelona, Mies synthesized conflicting themes. The space was continuous and centrifugal, but it was no longer the infinite space of the brick villa project — the positioning of certain walls, or screens, in relation to the edge of the podium imposed a limit.

Barcelona and Tugendhat were criticized for their luxurious elegance. In 1930, Mies warned that technical progress would lead to a loss of meaning in architecture:

Let us not overestimate the question of mechanization, standardization and rationalization.
And let us accept the changed economic and social conditions as fact. All these things go their destined way, blind to values.

The decisive thing is which of these given facts we choose to emphasize. This is where spiritual problems begin. The important question to ask is not "what?" but "how?"
That we produce goods and by what means we manufacture them means nothing spiritually speaking.
Whether we build high or low, with steel and glass, tells us nothing about the value of building.
Whether in town planning we aim at centralization or decentralization is a practical question, not one of value.
Yet it is the question of value that is decisive.
We have to establish new values, to demonstrate ultimate aims, in order to acquire standards or criteria.
For the meaning and right of every age, including our own, consists solely in giving the spirit the opportunity to exist.[14]

The Barcelona Pavilion, along with Le Corbusier's Villa Savoie (Poissy, 1929–31), marked the culmination and the close of the heroic period of modern architecture in Europe. Barcelona was acclaimed a masterpiece of modern architecture and an outstanding example of artistic achievement.

In the summer of 1930 Mies took over from Hannes Meyer at the Dessau Bauhaus. In its short history the Bauhaus moved twice: from Weimar to Dessau and from Dessau to Berlin.

Gropius set out the first Bauhaus Program in 1919:

The ultimate aim of all the visual arts is the complete building! To embellish buildings was once the noblest function of the fine arts . . . . Today the arts exist in isolation, from which they can be rescued only through the conscious, cooperative effort of all craftsmen.
Architects, sculptors, painters, we must all return to the crafts! For art is not a profession.
There is no essential difference between the artist and the craftsman.

Bauhaus teaching methods were linked to craft training, to the acquisition of craftsmanship, and as a teaching discipline it implied learning by doing. The innovation of the Bauhaus, over established methods of *Kunstgewerbeschule* training, lay in the introduction of handicraft methods to fine arts instruction.

The other great innovation was the *Vorkurs*, or preliminary course, which set out to cleanse each student's mind of all preconceptions. The Bauhaus *Vorkurs* acquired such fame that it came to be regarded as the essence, sometimes the entirety, of the Bauhaus Method.

When the school changed direction in 1923, the Bauhaus Method of instruction was easily adapted to the new approach. In *Idee und Aufbau*

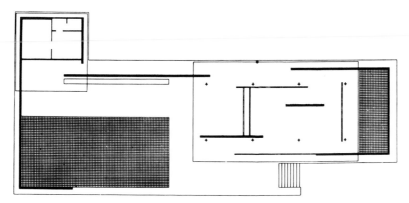

Ludwig Mies van der Rohe, German Pavilion, Barcelona. 1929. Plan. Courtesy of Museum of Modern Art.

des Staatlichen Bauhauses Weimar,[15] Gropius elaborated on the educational system:

The objective of all creative effort in the visual arts is to give form to space. But what is space and how can it be given form?
The brain conceives of mathematical space in terms of numbers and dimensions. The hand masters matter through the crafts, and with the help of tools and machinery. Conception and visualization are always simultaneous....
True creative work can only be done by the man whose knowledge and mastery of statics, dynamics, optics and acoustics equip him to give life and shape to his inner vision. In a work of art the laws of the physical world, the intellectual world and the world of the spirit function and are expressed simultaneously....
The guiding principle of the Bauhaus was therefore the idea of creating a new unity through the welding together of many arts and technology: a unity having its basis in Man himself and significant only as a living organism.
The human achievement depends on the proper coordination of all the creative faculties. It is not enough to school one or another of them separately: they must all be thoroughly trained at the same time.

The course was divided into two halves: *Werklehre* and *Formlehre*. The split was surprising, coming straight after the preamble which insisted on unity. However, in the interests of the new unity, Gropius brought the two disciplines closer by appointing studio masters equally proficient at both *Werklehre* and *Formlehre*. In practice this proved difficult.
Gropius then listed the various Bauhaus departments, but neither building nor architecture was given a department. Under the section Instruction in Architecture, he asserted:

Only the journeyman who has been seasoned by workshop practice and instruction in the study of form is ready to collaborate in building.
The last and most important stage of the Bauhaus education is the course in architecture, with practical experience in the Research Department as well as on actual buildings under construction.
In so far as the Bauhaus curriculum does not provide advanced courses in engineering — construction in steel and reinforced concrete, statics, mechanics, physics, industrial methods, heating, plumbing, technical chemistry — it is considered desirable for promising architecture students ... to complete their education with courses at technical and engineering schools.

Up until 1927, when a Bauhaus Department of Building was formed by Hannes Meyer, students of architecture gained experience only in Gropius's private practice.
Students had campaigned for an architecture department since 1923, when it became clear that no commissions would be forthcoming from the City of Weimar nor from its citizens. Since its beginning the Bauhaus

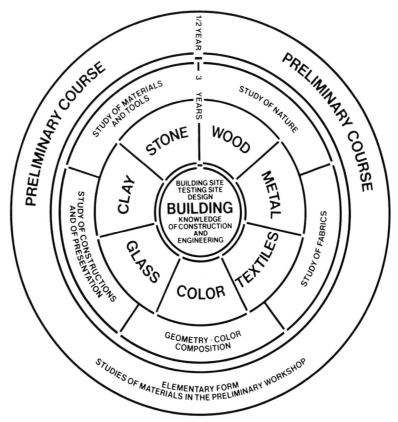

Educational Process at the Bauhaus, diagram. c.1919.

THE CURRICULUM

The course of instruction at the Bauhaus is divided into:

I.   Instruction in crafts (Werklehre):

STONE	WOOD	METAL	CLAY	GLASS	COLOR	TEXTILES
Sculpture workshop	Carpentry workshop	Metal workshop	Pottery workshop	Stained glass workshop	Wall-painting workshop	Weaving workshop

A.   Instruction in materials and tools

B.   Elements of book-keeping, estimating, contracting

II.   Instruction in form problems (Formlehre):

1. Observation	2. Representation	3. Composition
A. Study of nature	A. Descriptive geometry	A. Theory of space
B. Analysis of materials	B. Technique of construction	B. Theory of color
	C. Drawing of plans and building of models for all kinds of constructions	C. Theory of design

A Curriculum of the Bauhaus. c.1919.

had been unpopular in conservative Weimar; Gropius was accused of sheltering left-wing political activists. In 1922 Oscar Schlemmer's manifesto for the first Bauhaus exhibition referred to the Bauhaus as a "cathedral of socialism." From then on, both the architectural style developing in the school and the ideas of its faculty and students were attacked as leftist and communist. In 1925 the right-wing provincial government expelled the Bauhaus from Weimar.

When Meyer joined the Bauhaus in Dessau he criticized the education it offered. On taking over from Gropius (Mies refused the appointment), he found himself in a tragi-comic situation where, as head of the Bauhaus, he fought against Bauhaus style. Meyer attempted to put the architectural course on solid scientific foundations, and introduced fundamental changes into the curriculum. He invited Ludwig Hilberseimer to form a department of town planning and engaged Mart Stam to teach architecture. Alcar Rudelt and Friedrich Engemann were brought into teach structural engineering, and Walter Peterhans taught photography. Moholy-Nagy resigned, and Josef Albers took over the *Vorkurs* as well as teaching interior design.

Meyer's program for the Bauhaus aimed essentially at closer contact between the course of instruction and the needs and reality of life outside:

Building is a biological process. Building is not an aesthetic process. In its design the new dwelling becomes not only a "machine for living," but also a biological apparatus serving the needs of the mind and body.

He then gave a long list of "new age" synthetic materials and continued,

We organize these materials into a constructive whole based on economic principles. Thus the individual shape, the body of the structure, the color of the material and the surface texture evolve by themselves and are determined by life.

And he ended,

Building is nothing but organization: social, technical, economic, psychological organization.

Meyer's rejection of aesthetics, like Mies's, had qualifications: he is said to have been caught, on occasion, weighing the proportions of a building. In *Beton als Gestalter* published in 1928, Hilberseimer stated:

The rapid perfection of scientific methods of research and technical aids... caused, for a whole epoch an overestimation of the possibilities of technol-

ogy.... Technique is never more than a means for the art of building.... Technique and art are profoundly different.

He clearly separated the physical from the spiritual sciences.

After three hectic years Meyer was dismissed from the Bauhaus following pressure from the City Council of Dessau. Again Gropius invited Mies to head the Bauhaus, and this time he accepted.

Mies van der Rohe altered the character of the Bauhaus, and spiritually the real Bauhaus ended with Meyer's dismissal. The political and social activities characteristic of that illustrious era were virtually eliminated and, under Mies, the Bauhaus became a school of architecture. On his appointment there was protest from students who declaimed Mies as a builder of mansions. He closed the school and expelled the ringleaders of the revolt. He also closed the Prellerhaus to student residents, and they had to find lodgings elsewhere in Dessau.

There were faculty changes too, notably the appointment of Lilly Reich as lecturer. In January 1932 she succeeded Alfred Arndt in the interior design department. Hilberseimer taught architecture and town planning. Rudelt and Engemann continued to teach structural engineering. Mies retained Josef Albers (preliminary course, representational drawing), Wassily Kandinsky (introduction to artistic design), Hinnerk Scheper (wall painting), Joost Schmidt (woodworking), Walter Peterhans (photography) and Lyonel Feininger (master without formal appointment). Thus there was a large measure of continuity in teaching methods.

Mies's heavy-handed manner in dealing with unrest caused resentment among the students. Discontent led to infighting and occasionally strikes. His leadership was criticized, but he succeeded in quieting local ition to the school in Dessau and gained the support of the Mayor. Gropius had placed the Bauhaus in safe hands.

The Bauhaus gave him his first opportunity to teach. He took charge of final year architecture students and held seminars three days a week, mornings and afternoons. No papers were written, no examinations given. Students were assessed on architectural work alone.

Mies started his students designing houses. The first problem he set was a single-bedroom court-house. He said that if an architect could design a house well he could do almost anything. Students produced sketch after sketch — Mies recommended at least a hundred — then Mies would examine them at length and remark, more often than not, "*Versuchen Sie es wieder*" (try it again). When the scheme was finally approved it would be drawn. To reach this stage would take weeks, or even months.

One of Mies's students, Selman Selmanagic, drew a delightful comment on his project: "Selman," said Mies, "We shall have to start all over again." The student was surprised and started explaining eagerly how well the plan functioned. "Come now, Selman, if you meet twin sisters who are equally healthy, intelligent and wealthy, and both can bear children, but one is ugly, the other beautiful — which one would you marry?"[16]

Howard Dearstyne, an American student at the Bauhaus, wrote home at the end of 1931:

We are learning a tremendous lot from Mies van der Rohe. If he doesn't make good architects of us he'll at least teach us to judge what good architecture is. One of the uncomfortable (perhaps) sides of associating with an architect of the first rank is that he ruins your taste for about all but one–half of one percent of all the architecture that's being done the world over. Mies van der Rohe not only comes down hard on the American architects (for which he has, without the shadow of a doubt, the most perfect justification), but holds that one doesn't need the fingers of one hand to count the German architects who are doing good work.[17]

Ludwig Hilberseimer was the second architecture master, and he and Mies shared a Master House at the Bauhaus. They retained their architectural practices in Berlin and came to an arrangement whereby they commuted from Berlin alternately: Mies spending half the week in Dessau, and Hilberseimer the other half. Unlike Mies, Hilberseimer seemed a true Bauhäusler and his seminars, conducted in characteristic Bauhaus fashion, were more relaxed than Mies's. Pius Pahl, who studied under both masters, gave his impression:

I enter the room in which the lectures are given and sit down a little way from the others. They come in one by one and find places on tables, benches, stools and window–seats. They debate. I am waiting for Hilbs, but in vain. After some time one of the older students is addressed as Hilbs. What a surprise for a former student of the Höheres Staatliches Technikum![18]

For just over a year after Mies's take over relative calm reigned at the Bauhaus in Dessau. The political situation changed suddenly at the beginning of 1932 when the National Socialists gained a majority in the City Council of Dessau. The National Socialist candidates promised in their campaign to dissolve the Bauhaus and demolish its frame buildings. In October 1932, some staff, students and equipment moved to Berlin and the Bauhaus was for the third and last time in a new home. In

less than six months the Bauhaus died of attrition. Its financial support from Dessau ended, and on 11 April 1933, the Gestapo arrested some of the students, searched the building, sealed it and placed it under guard. As a school, the Bauhaus effectively ended, but as an institution the efforts of Mies and others continued, and it was not until 20 July 1933, that the faculty, consisting of Mies, Albers, Hilberseimer, Kandinsky, Peterhans, Reich and Walther unanimously voted to close the Bauhaus because of insufficient funds.

The three lives of the Bauhaus, Weimar, Dessau, Berlin, parallel the rise and fall of the Weimar Republic. It was a time of revolution, foreign occupation, political murder, fantastic inflation, seemingly endless experimentation in the arts, poverty and great wealth, vast unemployment, new architecture, manifestoes and general political violence culminating in government by decree. Culture became less the critic more the mirror of events. The newspaper and film industries ground out left- and right-wing propaganda, and the country was inundated by kitsch, much of it politically inspired.

Following Adolph Hitler's accession to power in the spring of 1933, his government began an attack on architects, depriving some of commissions and pressuring others from positions of leadership in professional organizations. The *Werkbund* was purged and a new council selected. A frequent visitor to Berlin in the 1930's, Philip Johnson analyzed the three factions involved in the struggle for control of the new Kulturpolitik. He said Mies was respected by conservatives like Paul Schmitthenner and that the *Kampfbund für Deutsche Kultur* (an organization set up in 1928 by Alfred Rosenburg) had nothing against him.

Johnson knew Mies had been awarded a prize (along with five others) for his entry in the Reichsbank Competition of February 1933. Mies's design was the only modern entry to win a prize — was monumental, stark and heavy, with rigidly ordered interiors. Johnson speculated that if (and it may be a long if) Mies should build this building it would clinch his position as the new Party architect.[19]

Joseph Goebbels, yet to declare his policy, was first unsympathetic to the opponents of modern art and architecture. He wished the new State to appear creative rather than restrictive. He attacked Rosenburg's *Kampfbund* and, in April 1933, promised artists freedom to create art suitable for the new regime. In November 1933 Goebbels set up the *Reichskulturkammer*, which became the only legal representative for creative professionals. It assumed control over the arts, and Goebbels

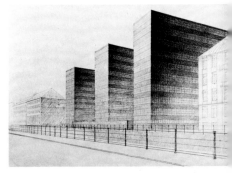

Ludwig Mies van der Rohe, Reichsbank Project, Berlin. 1933. Drawing. Courtesy of Hedrich Blessing.

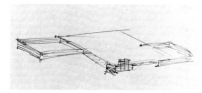

Ludwig Mies van der Rohe, Courthouse. c.1934. Sketch. Courtesy of Museum of Modern Art.

Ludwig Mies van der Rohe, Administration Building for the Silk Industry, Krefeld. 1937. Drawing. Main Hall.

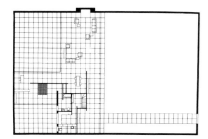

Ludwig Mies van der Rohe, House with Three Courts Project. 1934. Plan. Courtesy of Museum of Modern Art.

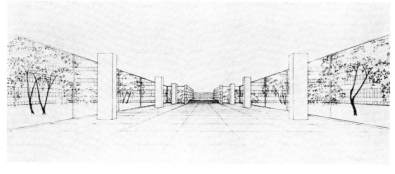

appointed the president of each chamber. By 1934 some artists who had portrayed the more exuberant spirit of the 1920's were listed as "degenerate" and their work was suppressed and banned from publication.

Gropius and Wagner hoped for support from Goebbels as late as June 1934. Häring defended the *Ring* as a professional organization of Prussian origin, rooted in the prewar *Werkbund*. Their efforts were fruitless; disillusion replaced hope and Gropius, who inspired and initiated appeals to the *Reichskulturkammer* began preparations to leave Germany. Mies, possibly the least political of the radical architects, seems to have kept a low profile after his negotiations with Rosenburg over the fate of the Berlin Bauhaus.

Mies, like Gropius, received commissions from the new government. For the propagandistic *Deutsches Volk/Deutsche Arbeit* exhibition of 1934, Mies designed the Glass and Mining exhibits, in which he displayed some of his tubular steel furniture. Gropius also designed an exhibit, while Cesar Klein designed the Nazi eagle tapestry, and Herbert

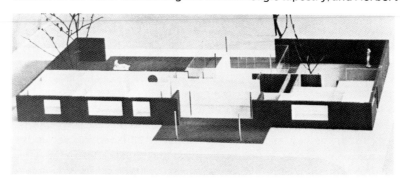

Ludwig Mies van der Rohe, Hubbe House, Magdeburg. 1935. Model. Courtesy of the Museum of Modern Art.

Bayer designed the catalogue. None of their names appeared, since they were elsewhere listed as degenerate artists.

In 1934 Mies entered the competition to design the national pavilion for the International Exhibition in Brussels. Later, Mies told his grandson, Dirk Lohan, that he heard that Hitler was so disgusted with his design that he threw it on the floor and stomped on it. In the years before his departure to America, Mies spent much of his time in the Tyrol, in Upper Bozen, but he stayed in contact with his Berlin office and Lilly Reich.

Mies's income after the closure of the Bauhaus came mostly from his furniture patents and, through Lilly Reich, from some small interior design commissions in Berlin. He continued to teach in his Berlin studio, and in August 1933 he took four students to Lugano for three months's tuition. Lilly Reich joined him there as did two American students, the former Bauhäusler Howard Dearstyne and John Rodgers. Until 1937 Mies employed two ex-Bauhaus students Eduard Ludwig and Herbert Hirche part-time. Ludwig executed the drawings for the Reichsbank Competition and the projected Administration Building for the Silk Industry in Krefeld — a building on a splayed plan similar to the Reichsbank. Mies was in America when this project was presented in Krefeld in 1937.

In the 1930's Mies studied the pavilion and the court — the theme of Barcelona. He repeated it in his Model House at the Berlin Building Exposition of 1931 — his last exhibition for the *Werkbund*. In the Model House, the flowing space still reached outward, channeled by screens, two of which slide out beyond the podium.

From 1931 to 1938, Mies developed a series of court–house projects in which the space, though still allowed to flow, was limited by the external walls of the house and court conjoined. Walls, glass and columns were used as progressively more subtle and more economic means of controlling space. Mies introduced the court–house theme to his students; it was a major topic at the Bauhaus and later at the Illinois Institute of Technology, where he produced montages of the schemes he had designed in Germany.

The sketches and montages enabled Mies to transcend material constraints and express his guiding intention more clearly. External views were selected and controlled by openings in the walls. Finally these openings were virtually eliminated. The houses became completely introspective, and their isolation may suggest Mies's need to shield himself from the reality of life in Germany.

The interiors were marked by their vacancy, occasionally filled by a sculpture, a painting, or a view, set against the unrelenting ascetic purity of walls and screens. The enclosed space contained the ideal of a monastic life, a private world where, surrounded by order and clarity, men could meditate on eternal truth and contemplate beautiful objects.

In August 1937, four years after he closed the Bauhaus and completed his last work in Germany, Mies was invited to America by Mr. and Mrs. Stanley Resor to design a dwelling in Wyoming. Mies was again invited to direct the architecture school of the Armour Institute of Technology, and this time he accepted. He visited Chicago then went back to New York to work on the Resor house and the Armour curriculum in the office of John Rodgers and William Priestley. With their help, and that of Howard Dearstyne, Mies drew up a program of architectural education based on his experience at the Bauhaus.

During the years of relative inactivity in Berlin Mies continued reading, including St. Augustine, St. Thomas Aquinas, and Spinoza. Later in the United States he quoted frequently from these writers, and they seemed to give him the inner strength he needed to live and work in a foreign land. He admired the writing of Romano Guardini, a contemporary philosopher whose book, *Das Ende der Neuzeit: Ein Versuch zur Orientierung*,[20] he recommended to his students.

During his last years in Germany Mies had time to think and develop his architectural philosophy of order and clarity which was reflected in the simplicity of the court–house projects. The architect he admired most was Rudolf Schwarz, a Roman Catholic whose book, *The Church Incarnate; The Sacred Function of Christian Architecture*, was translated into English and published in 1958 with Mies's help. In the Foreword, Mies wrote:

This book was written in Germany's darkest hour, but it throws light for the first time on the question of church building, and illuminates the whole question of architecture itself.

Rudolf Schwarz, the great German church builder, is one of the most profound thinkers of our time. His book, in spite of its clarity, is not easy reading — but he who will take the trouble to study it carefully will gain real insight into the problems discussed. I have read it over and over again, and I know its power of clarification. I believe it should be read not only by those concerned with church building but by anyone sincerely interested in architecture. Yet it is not only a great book on architecture, indeed it is one of the truly great books — one of those which have the power to transform our thinking.[21]

A difficulty with Mies is that what he said often seems to be at odds with what he did. But this is because he is easily taken too literally — both his words and his work. He set out to teach architecture as poetry. First the building had to be based on the clarity of its structural elements. To Mies this did not mean that the building had to express its structure in the literal sense of the functionalist school.

Mies's architecture was rooted in tradition, and developed in the Berlin of the 1920's. He saw clearly the nature of the era he lived in, and his work confirmed, interpreted and commented on some of the viable and meaningful thoughts of that era. He had the strength of his convictions, and the leadership to put them over.

Everyone looked at Ludwig Mies van der Rohe hoping he would tell them what to do — but he could only show them how to do it.

NOTES

1 Excerpts from Mies van der Rohe's Inaugural Address to the Armour Institute of Technology, Chicago, 1938 (complete text in Philip Johnson, *Mies van der Rohe*, 1978, pp. 196-200).
2 Ibid.
3 Ibid.
4 "Über Kunstkritik," *Das Kunstblatt*, 14, 1930, p. 178, translation in Johnson, p. 196.
5 Peter Carter, "Mies van der Rohe," *Architectural Design*, March 1961, p. 97.
6 "Mies Speaks," *Architectural Review*, December 1968, p. 451.
7 Carter, *AD*.
8 "Hochhausprojekt für Bahnhof Friedrichstrasse in Berlin," *Frühlicht*, No. 1, 1922, pp. 122-124, translated in Johnson, p. 187.
9 "Baukunst und Zeitwille," *Der Querschnitt*, No. 4, 1924, pp. 31–32.
10 "Bürohaus," *G*, No. 1, 1923, p. 32.
11 Peter Carter, *Mies at Work*, 1974, p. 18.
12 "Industrielles Bauen," *G*, No. 3, 1924, pp. 8–11. (Mies illustrated his article with a station building by Breest & Co., Berlin, and a factory building by Behrens, in collaboration with the same firm.)
13 "Rundschau: Zum Neuen Jahrgang," *Die Form*, Vol. 2, No 1, 1927, p. 1.
14 "Die Neue Zeit: Schlussworte des Referats Mies van der Rohe auf der Wiener Tagung des Deutschen Werkbundes," *Die Form*, Vol. 5, No. 15, 1930, p. 406, (slightly different translation in Johnson, p. 195).
15 J. Walter Gropius, *Idee und Aufbau des Staatlichen Bauhauses Weimar*, Munich & Weimar: Bauhaus Verlag, 1923, p. 12; reprinted in *Staatliches Bauhaus Weimar 1919-1923*, Munich & Weimar: Bauhaus Verlag, 1923, p. 226.
16 Pius Pahl, "Experiences of an Architectural Student," *Bauhaus and Bauhaus People*, Ed. Eckhard Neumann, 1970, p. 229.
17 Howard Dearstyne, "Mies van der Rohe's Teaching at the Bauhaus in Dessau," *Bauhaus and Bauhaus People*, Ed. Eckhard Neumann, p. 213.
18 Pahl, p. 228.
19 Philip Johnson, "Architecture and the Third Reich," *Hound and Horn, VII*, Oct.–Dec. 1933, pp. 137–139. (reprinted in Philip Johnson, *Writings*, 1979, p. 53.)
20 Romano Guardini, *Das Ende der Neuzeit: Ein Versuch zur Orientierung*, Basel, 1950.
21 Rudolf Schwarz (Cynthia Harris, translator), *The Church Incarnate; The Sacred Function of Christian Architecture*, Chicago, 1958.

ORDER, SPACE, PROPORTION — MIES'S CURRICULUM AT IIT

Kevin Harrington

When Ludwig Mies van der Rohe (1886–1969) arrived in Chicago in 1938 to begin his career as the director of the architecture program at Armour (later Illinois) Institute of Technology, his experience in education was both extensive and brief. As with his architecture up to that time, his educational experience showed very great promise and relatively little actual achievement.

Nonetheless, when he took up his duties in Chicago, he had already been the first choice to be head of architecture at Harvard University, and his importance was eloquently acknowledged by Paul Cret of the University of Pennsylvania and inelegantly confirmed by Frank Lloyd Wright.

Mies proclaimed his importance and ideals to Americans initially in two key statements: the speech he gave at a welcoming dinner in October 1938, and in the curriculum he had earlier developed and begun implementing that same fall at Armour. The speech, which Mies saw as an occasion similar to the address given in many universities when a new professor takes his chair, was stirring and quickly and widely reprinted. The curriculum was revolutionary. It established a method of work, analysis, and design which sought to imbue brick, glass, steel and space with a coherent and rational expression. Juxtaposing an architecture of space and frame, Mies wanted to create a curriculum which would always yield excellent craftsmen and occasionally produce or encourage those with the gifts to make the expression of technique an act of high art.

Reflecting his interest in crystal structure, Mies was after a curriculum which would encourage students to seek and find that moment when the crystalline essence of a problem or idea was revealed. Thus students began by drawing lines, to learn their weight, shape, space and nature; then they began studying intersections of lines, learning the complex set of interrelationships among the parts; then they began studying materials in order to search out the moment when two bricks might become architecture; then the intersecting lines of two dimensions would be extended to three dimensions in an effort to understand space, the most important and difficult element of the entire esthetic. Only then, when a student had mastered the elements of architecture, from the particularity of a single well drawn line to the ineffable development of the perfect space, would a student attempt to solve the problem of an actual building.

This idea — to create a line, a plane, a space, a building so complete that nothing could be added or subtracted — marks Mies's adherence to one of the central ideas of what is called the classical tradition. Vitruvius and Alberti defined beauty in such terms and their presence in Mies's thought demonstrates the broad circle of tradition upon which he drew. While Mies expected his undergraduates to be able to leave school knowing how to speak the language of modern architecture, in the graduate program he hoped to attract and teach those whose gifts might allow them occasionally to make poetry of that language.

The hiring of Mies by Armour Institute in 1937 followed a two year courtship which was interrupted by the attraction of Harvard. Several elements combined to bring Armour to make itself an acceptable position for the world renowned architect.

Armour's architecture program had been without effective leadership for some time. Earl H. Reed directed a program organized around the competitions of the Beaux-Arts Institute of Design in New York. Also offered were a number of courses that took Chicago's distinctive character for its subject, including steel structure, the tall building, and the local building code. Competent to instruct and criticize the students, and handle the day to day management of the program, Reed could not lead. From the late 1920's when asked to reshape the curriculum, Reed acknowledged the usefulness of such an action, yet proved unable to develop any sure analysis and program for the future.

During this time, members of the administration discovered two things as the depression continued. First enrollment was actually rising, and second, they had a larger enrollment than any other urban engineering school. Of special interest were the comparable enrollment figures for the Massachusetts and California Institutes of Technology, which were lower than those at Armour. Within the Armour administration were a number of relatively young and ambitious men who sought to create in Chicago a technological center the equal of the two more prestigious institutions on the east and west coasts.

Armour had already spent some years exploring transforming itself. In the 1920's, Armour reached an agreement with Northwestern University to become its engineering school and move into its new Lake Shore Drive campus. When Armour could not secure its share of the funding, the administration decided to rely no longer on the gifts of a few private donors and instead sought funding from industrialists through their corporations. This decision rested in the belief that the Institute and industry could work cooperatively to their mutual benefit, and that the research and development the Institute offered would have rapid and profitable impact on the industries and their competitiveness.

Although the corollary of this decision for architecture would be to focus the school on the Chicago region, and although in its earliest days the school officially had been called the Chicago School of Architecture, there was not any parallel discussion of Chicago's special architectural character. Students described the enervation of the architecture school as weak leadership and desultory teaching.

In July 1935, Burton Buchhauser reported to Dean Henry Heald the conversations of four students,

... every man of worth, every genius, and intellectual giant had a great person for his guiding light, his teacher or close friend. Frank Lloyd Wright had Louis Sullivan, Sullivan had H. H. Richardson, and A.I.T. Arx graduates have heavy hearts, ... instructors at A.I.T. have laughed at me for suggesting F. L. W.'s name and principles as my inspiration.

I am starting at the top and working my way down through the group, and all those I criticize I have had personal contact, and felt the shallow influence of. The head of the department is the perfect example of what we can do without. ... He frequents the drafting rooms ... as a floor walker overlooking the merchandise.

... He is a diplomat to the *nth* degree, accomplishing absolutely nothing for anyone, reaping his yearly harvest, and at the same time performing a peculiar hiding act .... He, is nothing but the old charlatan creeping into a field too honest to approve his dealings.

I have received a statement made by him that no power could move him from his position if he saw fit to remain — his drag with the trustees is to hold him secure. How do I know so many peculiar details? I worked for one year in his office as student assistant and know the daily rape he has made on the school and its trust in him.

The junior crit lacks the same qualities that the senior crit forgot to acquire. Lack of interest for a young man's problems; lack of time spent in the class rooms; criticisms which are of little use because of the short time spent with each man; a mind on outside pleasures; a wild glare in his eye which tells of distant thought; and last but not least a personality too distant to be reached by the trying student.

To close, I shall say it possible to create the things I demand and expect for the future Arx, as they all existed under the leadership of Professor Campbell, a former dean at A.I.T.[1]

Heald's sympathy towards the students developed from his own experience and teaching. He had taught concrete construction both to engineers and architects, and he described how much he enjoyed teaching the architects.

In September 1935, Heald prepared a "Memorandum Regarding Architecture at Armour Institute of Technology." In it he identified three areas of concern. The first two, dealing with curriculum and faculty, he recognized as the responsibility of the Institute, although it would not be easy to reform the curriculum quickly. His third proposal, to form a committee of outside professional architects to observe and advise the department and administration, initiated an analysis of the current program to determine the best future for the school.

The architects selected for this committee, all in practice in Chicago, were Alfred Alschuler, C. Herrick Hammond, John Holabird, Jerrold Loebl, and Alfred Shaw. Alschuler, Hammond and Loebl were Armour alumni. As an Armour Trustee, Alschuler was the Mr. Inside, while Holabird was Mr. Outside. Further, each was loyal to and supportive of Earl Reed, so that, at least at the outset, neither Reed, nor his faculty, need have felt disconcerted by the formation of the committee.

Asked for an analysis of the situation, Reed prepared a very long description of a fairly typical architectural curriculum, demonstrating neither a grasp of the problem nor any clear ideas for the future. Early in 1936, Willard Hotchkiss, Armour's president, wrote Holabird that,

. . . the work ahead was both short range and long range and that we welcome advice on the immediate matters pointed to in [Reed's] report, but that we are particularly desirous of laying down the groundwork of a long-time program which would result in a school of architecture much more worthy of Chicago than at present . . . . I think you know, this is exactly my idea, and the reason for creating a committee of cooperating architects, under your chairmanship . . .[2]

Hotchkiss included a new memorandum Heald had prepared. Heald had concluded Reed was unable to address the problems of the school.

. . . Mr. Reed's report summarizes in considerable detail the work of the Department and will serve as the source of adequate information as to present conditions, but the Committee can probably be of maximum service by approaching the problem as a broad assignment to prepare complete specifications for an outstanding Department of Architecture of from 75 to 100 students for Chicago.[3]

Holabird got to work in February, writing a number of architects for advice.[4] They responded by urging the selection of a strong, energetic, young head with the ability and opportunity to implement his ideas. A list of younger men was drawn up, and Holabird wrote them asking if they knew anyone prepared for such a challenge.[5]

In March he wrote to Mies, saying that Armour wanted,

. . . the best available head . . . with the idea of making it the finest school in this Country.
I . . . have canvassed . . . various American architects . . . Amongst others . . . Richard Neutra . . . He suggested . . . Walter Gropius or Josef Emanuel Margold as he felt the best was none too good for Chicago . . . .
In talking the matter over with the Advisory Committee, I thought that as we were considering the possibility of a European heading this school that I would like to ask if you would, under any conditions, consider such an appointment. I am, of course, a great admirer of your work and if we are to consider the best I would naturally turn to you first.[6]

Noting that Paul Cret in Philadelphia and Eliel Saarinen in Detroit had combined teaching successfully with practice, Holabird assured Mies of that opportunity in Chicago, suggesting a salary between $8,000 and $10,000 per year.

In 1936 Mies's knowledge of Chicago was general and circumstantial. On the general level would be Mies's professional knowledge of archi-tects and architecture associated with Chicago. Erich Mendelsohn's *Amerika* of 1927 or Richard Neutra's *Wie Baut Amerika* of 1926, which presented Chicago and its buildings, or Mies's memory of Frank Lloyd Wright would have reminded him of architecture of significance and interest in Chicago.

Circumstantially the exhibition of "Modern Architecture" at the Museum of Modern Art in 1932, treated Mies with great respect, ranking him with Gropius, Oud and Le Corbusier. The exhibition catalog also included a brief history of modern architecture which traveled through Chicago by way of Richardson, Sullivan and Wright. Richard Neutra, presented as an example of a European experiencing success in America, had moved to that success through Chicago and the Holabird & Roche office. The youngest native born American architects in the exhibition, the Bowman brothers, Irving and Monroe, graduates of Armour, had earlier worked for Holabird & Root, and the catalog compared their work to Mies. His colleague and friend, Ludwig Hilberseimer, also discussed the work of Holabird & Root in his books.

When Mies received Holabird's letter, he recognized the name, firm, school and city. In a cable of 20 April, followed by a letter of 4 May, Mies expressed interest in the position, asking for more information on the curriculum, facilities, and opportunity for private practice.

Armour replied quickly, with a letter of 12 May,[7] followed by cables from Hotchkiss on 4 June and Holabird on 11 June. Armour's ardor derived from learning that Joseph Hudnut, the new dean at Harvard, expressed interest in Mies's taking the chair in architecture at the Graduate School of Design. This effort coincided with an attempt to retain Mies as the design architect for the Museum of Modern Art.[8] Alfred Barr saw Mies on 20 June 1936, bringing messages of Hudnut and the Museum of Modern Art. Mies expressed interest in both opportunities. The other architects Barr contacted on the matter, Oud and Gropius, answered both questions, respectively, with a no and a maybe.

On the same day, 20 June, that Mies received Barr with enthusiasm, he wrote Armour with reservations about its program, saying that no simple reform of the existing program would suit him, and that a proper curriculum must address both the

. . . premises, nature and forms of expression of earlier cultures [and] the structure of our own . . . in order to make clear the bases and the possibilities available for our own cultural work.

You will understand that I hesitated to take the proffered position since so far reaching and extensive an expansion of the present organization seemed to me difficult of execution. After thorough consideration I feel that I cannot accept your invitation, but I would be glad, should you desire, to name distinguished persons whom I consider valuable and capable to undertake the direction of the Department of Architecture of your Institute.[9]

Mies closed the door, but offering to suggest other names left it unlocked. In addition, his reply to Holabird, suggested the door might even be ajar:

I am very sorry to inform you that after thorough consideration I am unable to accept your invitation to Armour Institute.
I am doing this because it seems impossible to carry through in the available framework of the school the complicated and thorough education of architects, which nowadays seems necessary.
The changes in the system of education would have to be so fundamental that they would greatly overstep the present limits of the architectural department. I thank you very much for your efforts and hope your wishes and plans for the Institute will be fulfilled.[10]

As a fall back position, the second choice of the Advisory committee was the head of design at the University of Illinois, Arthur Deam. He had taught briefly at Armour before going to Illinois.[11]
When Heald realized that Hudnut sought Mies he saw his own thinking confirmed. Although Hudnut's curricular changes at Columbia aroused controversy, his proposals accorded with Heald's thinking and Mies's statements of principle in replying to Armour. As Heald was attempting at Armour, Columbia had established a committee of distinguished professionals to study the architecture school as it was. It also studied other programs, including Saarinen's at Cranbrook, as well as other American schools of architecture. This report concluded that,

These things we believe to be essential:
a. A flexible curriculum . . .
b. Elimination of competition . . .
c. Stimulation of creative instinct and logical thought . . .
d. A true relation between the various branches of study . . .
e. Contact with leaders of Architecture and of other professions . . .
Realizing the fundamental changes indicated in this report, we recommend that the Dean should have an absolutely free hand to effect them.[12]

Hudnut developed Columbia's curriculum with six major elements. First, the competition was abandoned and replaced by the "problem" method. Second, Problems were of two types. The Major Problem was individual, non-competitive and of open length, while the second,

Sketch, problems were to be done in groups on a competitive basis, of short duration. Third, problems in construction were required. Fourth, special talents of the student were recognized and encouraged. Fifth, the thesis was retained. Sixth, students could enter only one outside competition a year.[13]
The parallels between Hudnut's proposals and Mies's later suggestions, and their agreement with the thesis of these changes, confirmed Armour's desire to hire Mies.
The advisory committee saw some possibility of retaining Mies, for on 30 June, they rejected Deam, instead urging Armour to take another chance on Mies by inviting him to come to Chicago to study the situation for one or two weeks, and permit both sides to meet. In the interim they proposed conducting the school flexibly. They received Reed's resignation, leaving the school year 1936–1937, without a director, managed by Jerrold Loebl and Louis Skidmore.
In writing Mies, Hotchkiss emphasized the freedom available if he accepted Armour's offer:

It would be difficult, I believe, to find an educational situation which is essentially more flexible than ours. Our reason for wishing to interest you in becoming Director of our Department of Architecture was the belief that you would be able to chart a sound course for the future better than anyone else whom we had considered.[14]

Mies did not respond to Hotchkiss's letter until 2 September,

I have to inform you that in the meantime I have received an offer from another American university, which I am thinking of accepting.[15]

Here is a rare case of Mies's overstepping, as subsequent events made clear. Mies had not understood the conditional nature of his discussions with Hudnut. It also suggests that Mies did not see his practice or his person to be in any imminent danger in Germany. Although such Jews as Mendelsohn and non-Jews as Gropius had left, Mies's rejection of Armour indicates no need of an appointment for reasons of personal safety.
Mies learned from Barr, Hudnut's initial emissary, on 19 July that,

I have tried very hard to have our Museum bring you to America as collaborating architect on our new building, but I am afraid that I shall not succeed.
Believe me, I am very much disappointed in my defeat. It has been a hard battle. In any case I hope most sincerely for a favorable outcome to your conversation with Dean Hudnut.

With kindest regards to you and Miss Reich — it was, believe me, a great pleasure to see you again.[16]

Barr continued to try to get Mies the job at the Museum, but he did not write Mies again of this.

Mies could only have felt he had misunderstood Hudnut when he received Hudnut's letter of 3 September. When Hudnut left Mies in Berlin he may not have anticipated the effect Gropius, then in England, might have. As is said of Deans, Hudnut was the victim of the last person consulted, in this case Gropius. In writing Armour on 2 September that he had received an offer, Mies did not expect this from Hudnut:

My visit in Europe is ending . . . and I wish again to thank you for your many courtesies to me during my days in Berlin.
I should like . . . to make a formal request to the President of the University in respect to the appointment of a Professor of Design. I hope that I may receive from you a letter telling me that you are able to consider favorably the acceptance of a chair should this be offered you . . . . I do not suggest that you should accept the Chair before it is offered, and I assure you that your letter will in no way commit you to such a course.
It would be foolish to pretend that there will not be opposition to the appointment of a modern Architect as Professor of Design. In Berlin I tried to make clear to you the cause of this opposition — which is based in part on ignorance and in part on a difference in principles — and since my visit in Berlin, I have received letters which promise an opposition even more serious than I expected.
The President suggests that my chance of success may be improved if he is able to present to the Senate at least two names, each of which is acceptable to me.
I should like, therefore, to propose not only your name but also that of Mr. Gropius. If for any reason this does not meet with your approval, I hope you will tell me so frankly.
Will you kindly give my regards — and those of my wife — to Frau Reich?[17]

A letter of Mies's on 2 September, outlining his willingness to accept a Harvard appointment, and his interest in the conditions of professional practice must have crossed Hudnut's letter in the mail, for Mies wrote Hudnut on 15 September, that,

Your letter . . . forces me to the unpleasant decision to cut back the agreements I made to you in my letter of 2 September.
I am willing to accept an appointment, but not to make myself a candidate for a chair. If you stand by your intention to submit several names . . . kindly omit mine.[18]

To send this letter, Mies knew the Harvard position might be lost. Whether Hudnut deceived him, or his ambition exceeded his calcula-

tion, the flight of Harvard and MoMA made him wonder why Armour's offer escaped his grasp. As Mies considered Hudnut's letters of 28 September, 26 October, and 6 November he realized his chance had escaped him. Hudnut's tone becomes more businesslike, his suggestions of friendship disappear, and he reports secondary material. In the 28 September 1936, letter he declares:

It has not been, at any time, my intention to make it appear that you are a candidate for an appointment at Harvard and I have been most careful not to do anything which might lead any one to suppose that this was true.[19]

If this were true, it is impossible to understand Mies's declaring to Hotchkiss that he was considering accepting an offer.

In the 26 October letter, addressed to questions of practice, Mies learned both Barr and Hudnut had spoken in ignorance on matters they should have known. He had the choice of deciding them to be duplicitous or stupid. Neither was attractive:

Among those states which will permit no foreigner to practice architecture under any circumstances is the important state of New York. I am greatly surprised and greatly shocked by this circumstance which seems to me stupid and unfair . . . [It is not clear if Mies knew that prior to taking his position at Harvard, Hudnut had been dean at Columbia, and thus presumably in a position to know something of licensing procedures in New York.]
In Massachusetts a citizen of a foreign country may obtain a license to practice architecture, but such a license will permit him to undertake a commission for one building only . . . .
The third state in [architectural] importance is Illinois. In Illinois, qualified men from France, Germany, Austria, and Italy have been registered and been permitted to practice, even though they were not citizens of the United States.
The information which I have outlined above has caused me very great disappointment, not only because I am afraid that you will feel you cannot consider a Chair in a city in which you cannot practice, but also because it would prevent you from carrying on important work, were you to come here. It was not merely my plan to give you opportunities for teaching: I was almost equally interested in the service I might render the cause of architecture in this country.[20]

As Mies considered the ambiguities of being offered and not being offered the same job by the same person in the same letter, one view of the last paragraph is that Hudnut wished Mies to withdraw his candidacy, because Mies would not be in a position to realize Hudnut's purposes. On 6 November Hudnut reports being "greatly distressed by this delay, but I am not discouraged . . . ." He noted meeting Michael (whom he recalled as Martin) van Beuren, a student of Mies's at the

Bauhaus, urging van Beuren to write Mies frankly of the situation.[21] The letter of 16 November delivered the final blow:

I am sorry to have to write to you, after conferences with the President and with members of the Governing Boards, that I have not been successful in my plans. I think it will be impracticable to invite you at the present time to accept a Chair at Harvard. I believe it will be necessary for me to consider what other men may be available for appointment as Professor of Design. I feel that I ought to tell you this frankly.

I am very greatly disappointed, but I shall not give up the hope that, in the future, there may develop a situation in which it will be practicable for me to take up with you once more the plans which we discussed in Berlin.

Please be assured of my continued esteem and of my sincere gratitude to you — not only for your many courtesies to me in Berlin, but also for the generous consideration you have given me since the time of my visit there.[22]

A cordial letter, except it is compromised by a letter Hudnut wrote to Alfred Barr the same day:

I should like to tell you — of course in confidence — that it is highly probable that Gropius will be appointed Professor of Design in our school . . . It seems to me to be practicable, therefore, for you to make use of his services in New York, should you wish to do so.[23]

Hudnut seems not to remember what he wrote to Mies only three weeks earlier:

I felt so strongly in respect to the information [that you would not be permitted to practice even as a consultant in New York] given me by the Chairman of the [National Council of Architectural Registration] Board that I went so far as to ask my lawyers whether or not the position of the Board could be maintained in the courts, and I asked my friend, Mr. Barr, to address a similar question to his attorneys. In both instances we were informed that the law had already been tested . . . and the Board's position upheld by the court.[24]

If what he said then was true, what he said to Barr is silly and would give Barr pause, for he had attempted to have a foreign architect serve as a collaborator and lost, as well as having made inquiries on exactly this matter for Hudnut.

Despite Mies's rejection, Hotchkiss wrote back immediately:

I am pleased to know that you are likely to get to America in the spring, and shall hope that we can at least have you in Chicago for a lecture and that the members of our faculty and advisory committee will have the opportunity of your counsel, which you have so generously offered to make available.[25]

In acknowledging his copy of this letter, Holabird wrote Hotchkiss:

I am sorry to hear that he has decided to go to an Eastern university. I know that we made the first offer but in all probability whoever it is in the East offered him half again as much as we indicated. [Actually, Hudnut's memo on the subject set salary at $10,000 or 25% more than Armour.][26] I had hoped that he might spend a year or two here before receiving such an offer.

I will gather the Committee together to discuss the matter of the lecture. It seems to me much more important to decide whom you can get permanently for Head of the school. I must confess I hate to consider anyone but the top.[27]

A more important letter from Holabird to Hotchkiss reported that Mies was exploring whether the door that he again closed might be opened:

Yesterday Mr. Loebl introduced me to an American, M. Van Beuren, who has just returned from Germany where he spent two or three years studying with Mies van der Rohe. He said that he had translated our letters and knew all about his possible connection in this Country.

Harvard was the other university that made a proposition to him but it seems that there has been some hitch [!] and his status is, therefore, uncertain. He definitely declined your offer as at that time he realized that you had to have a definite answer although he as yet had not determined definitely the course he was going to pursue.

[Holabird then reported asking Mies to come and lecture, accepting van Beuren's warning that Mies could not speak English.]

Mr. Loebl had time to show him around the Art Institute and show him in detail the work of the school. Van Beuren seemed to think that this would be a logical place for him to come. Incidentally, he said that Mies van der Rohe was very quiet, agreeable personality, modest and a fine instructor. In his opinion the school here would be very successful.[28]

Reporting to Mies on his visit, as well as the advice of former Mies students, John Rodgers and William Priestley, van Beuren said,

[We] believe it is better for you in Chicago. The people have more initiative; they get more naturally and directly to the point . . . .

At Armour . . . the people repeated their promise of absolute freedom . . . .

But the school is small, . . . and the location is miserable . . . what an example it is of America's fantastic inconsistencies . . . .[29]

Hardly a ringing endorsement of Armour, yet the opportunity might be greater. Mies now had to consider whether he wished to create a school and curriculum, a process that would take enormous thought and work. At Harvard Mies would have been a not the professor of design. Even with the prestige the position afforded, the curriculum was Hudnut's responsibility. Among the ironies, Harvard would afford the most time for private practice, yet the Massachusetts laws prohibited it, and the responsibility at Armour would limit the time spent in private pursuits, although the licensing in Illinois permitted it.

Mies did not follow up on the inquiries made by van Beuren. He considered his options, refusing to make a precipitate move. Losing the opportunities at MoMA and Harvard, forced Mies to be deliberate in making his next move.

For its part, Armour wished to avoid a second school year without a director. Not having heard again from Mies, it negotiated with Deam of the University of Illinois. Even as they sought Deam, Hotchkiss and Holabird hoped to do better in the future.

When Deam declined the appointment, the Architect's Committee extended the pattern developed in the past year, with Charles Dornbusch as Senior Critic, in place of the often traveling Louis Skidmore, and Jerrold Loebl as Acting Director. As late as 22 July 1937, Armour discussed the future of the department without mention of Mies. They had heard neither from him nor such American contacts as van Beuren, Rodgers or Priestley.

Following an initial contact in February and interviews early that summer, Mies accompanied Helen Resor to America in August to see the site of the house they wished him to design. During the train layover in Chicago on 23 August, on the trip to the Resor's Wyoming site, Mies briefly saw the city, concentrating on Richardson, Sullivan and Wright, in the company of Priestley and two other architects. Priestley spoke to John Holabird who expressed keen interest in seeing Mies on his return from Wyoming.

On 9 September, Mies had lunch with John Holabird, Alfred Shaw, C. Herrick Hammond, Jerrold Loebl, Charles Dornbusch, Helmut Bartsch, William Priestley and Henry Heald. He visited the Art Institute and the 33rd Street campus. Heald reported to Hotchkiss that, "Mr. Holabird and the other architects are extremely enthusiastic about the prospect of getting Mies to become a member of the staff of our Department of Architecture."[30]

The next day, a Friday, Mies left for Taliesen to meet Frank Lloyd Wright. Intended as an overnight visit, the encounter extended until Monday.[31] At a luncheon on Tuesday with Heald and Armour's chairman of the Board of Trustees, James Cunningham, Mies was asked to prepare a curriculum, which he intended to complete in Chicago, but was forced to complete later in New York where he worked on the Resor project.

Mies made a good impression, and Armour did not wish to lose him a second time. Heald concluded his memo to Hotchkiss:

Mies van der Rohe appears to be a very excellent man. He has a pleasant personality and a fine appearance. At the present time, he cannot speak English, but I presume that could be remedied reasonably soon. He indicated that he was interested in our opportunity and that, in case something could be worked out, he might be available within six months or so.[32]

Hotchkiss wrote Mies on the 17th, requesting Mies to specify his curriculum, prior to offering his appointment. Replying to Hotchkiss on the 22nd, already back in New York, Mies expressed interest in the problem and the position. Instead of returning to Europe by mid-October, he spent the winter in New York, with a brief trip to Chicago in February, before leaving for Europe at the end of March.

On 10 December 1937, Mies sent Heald his description and chart of his curriculum for Armour. He delayed this proposal,

. . . to give myself time to acquire sufficient insight into American conditions to enable me to adjust my proposals more fully to the cultural situation here.
In contrast to the mastery of the material world and the high development in the technical and economic fields, the lack of a determining force in the cultural realm leads here to an uncertainty which can be overcome only through sufficient insight into spiritual relationships.
It would serve no useful purpose, therefore, to add another educational method to those already in existence, unless this, while providing as a matter of course the necessary professional training, were to lead without fail to a clear and unequivocal spiritual orientation.
For this reason I have undertaken to develop a curriculum which in itself incorporates this clarifying principle of order, which leaves no room for deviation and which, through its systematic structure, leads [to] an organic unfolding of spiritual and cultural relationships.
Inasmuch as the question is that of an organic principle of order, depending on no definite presuppositions but reckoning with given American conditions, the danger of grafting one form of culture on an environment of another character is avoided.
Culture cannot be imported but results from the harmonious unfolding of one's own powers.
The strength but also the difficulty in the American situation lies in the existence of new problems of spiritual significance and new means for their solution. But the strength of the existing organizational and technical forces assures the possibility of an original and meaningful solution of the cultural question.
Culture as the harmonious relationship of man to his environment and architecture as the necessary manifestation of this relationship is the meaning and goal of the course of studies.
Accompanying program is the unfolding of this plan. Step I is an investigation

into the nature of materials and their truthful expression. Step II teaches the nature of functions and their truthful fulfillment. Step III on the basis of these technical and utilitarian studies begins the actual creative work in architecture. Step by step, as the training progresses, the architectural problem will reveal itself in its fullness and monumentality.

The consistent execution of this plan, with the inclusion of the fine arts, terminates logically in a Universitas Artis.[33]

Insisting on the three step sequence from structure to plan to beauty, Mies distanced his curriculum from Gropius and the Bauhaus on one hand and the Beaux-Arts method on the other. For Gropius, architecture (delight) inevitably resulted from the correct solution of plan and structure.[34] For the Beaux-Arts method, the architect's first responsibility was to develop a clear form or *parti*, to which problems of organization and structure would be subordinate. If one assumed a masonry tradition, allowing for great flexibility in the *poché*, to resolve conflicting interests and forms, the Beaux-Arts system had great validity. Mies's application of the insight presented by Le Corbusier in his Dom-ino House, that the vertical frame and horizontal floor slabs were independent, to problems distinct from issues of function or *a priori* form led him to choose structure as the basis upon which architecture could be developed. For much of his career Mies studied books on crystal theory. In determining that structure, as idea and fact, provided the basis of modern architecture, he saw structure as analogous to the crystal structure at the base of all matter. Mies sought the crystalline basis of structure to learn to give it expression. He followed the "road of discipline from materials, through function, to creative work."[35] Architecture "is the crystallization of [time's] inner structure, the slow unfolding of its form."[36] Focusing on a question of values, Mies attempted to understand and communicate them reasoning by analogy.

In addition to his own ideas on education, Mies studied material in the contemporary American discussion of education and values. Mies collected and read several books on this debate in the late thirties. Throughout, he attempted to understand the Americanness of the problem. One of the key words which he emphasizes is organic. The several days Mies spent with Frank Lloyd Wright in September 1937 gave Mies the idea that organic was an appropriately American word, leading him to use it frequently to summarize his thinking about architectural education. Such was the case in preparing his prospectus for the educational program at Armour in the winter of 1937–1938.[37] Here

organic is used to mean coherent, consequential, related to an order. It does not assume a simple or primitive state.

Before making these points, Mies studied the debate in America about the role of the professional school in university education. His claim for a "universitas artis" at the end of his December letter is, in part, an effort to counter the objections of such academics as Robert Hutchins of the University of Chicago. Hutchins, whom Mies had studied to the point of underlining key passages,[38] argued that a professional school was training while a university should be concerned with values not technique, and so the two were inherently hostile. Mies's response, that the two were crucially interconnected is summarized in Paul Valery's *Eupalinos, or the Architect*, where Socrates apologizes for his prior emphasis on the mind,

If, then, the universe is the effect of some act; that act itself, the effect of a Being, and of a need, a thought, a knowledge and a power which belongs to that Being, it is then only by an act that you can rejoin the grand design, and undertake the imitation of that which has made all things. And that is to put oneself in the most natural way in the very place of the God.[39]

Mies's ideas on the learning process reflected his experience and study. At its core he believed one learned when one needed the material being taught. In addition to a low level of curiosity, it assumes as well a short time horizon. One learns the immediately useful or necessary, but has difficulty learning what may be useful in the future. Mies further believed that college students were not sufficiently experienced to consider larger questions in a meaningful manner. Instead, Mies sought to train his students so they could make good, safe buildings, believing they would not become creative until later when they began to question and explore what they had previously taken for granted.

This does not mean that Mies was unconcerned with the teaching of academic or non-professional subjects. In developing the curriculum, he gave much of the first year to non-professional studies so students would be aware of the role of and need for values in modern society. In addition, he asked that they be taught the academic tools, mathematics and physics, which he assumed supported his own architectural ideas. Since Mies did not have an academic background, his knowledge of physics and calculus was largely based on office experience and his own assumptions, reinforced by his readings in philosophy and science, that they provided a foundation for creative thought.

ARCHITECTURAL EDUCATION

PROGRAM FOR PROFESSIONAL TRAINING / GENERAL THEORY

MEANS

FORM
CREATION OF ELEMENTARY BUILDING FORMS
BASED ON AND INCLUDING DETAILING OF TYPES OF CONSTRUCTION IN

WOOD·STONE·BRICK·STEEL·CONCRETE

VARIOUS COMBINATIONS OF THE ABOVE MATERIALS

CONSTRUCTION
- DIFFERENT METHODS OF WOOD CONSTRUCTION
- DIFFERENT METHODS OF STONE CONSTRUCTION
- DIFFERENT METHODS OF BRICK CONSTRUCTION
- DIFFERENT METHODS OF STEEL CONSTRUCTION
- DIFFERENT METHODS OF CONCRETE CONSTRUCTION
- APPLICATION OF THESE MATERIALS IN VARIOUS TYPES OF CONSTRUCTION

MATERIAL
(For each material: WHERE AND HOW OBTAINED / HOW WORKED / PHYSICAL PROPERTIES / STRUCTURAL PROPERTIES / AESTHETIC QUALITIES)

- WOOD
- STONE
- BRICK
- STEEL
- CONCRETE
- FILLING, SURFACING, ENVELOPING AND OTHER MATERIALS

PURPOSES

INTERIOR FURNISHING
MATERIALS / CONSTRUCTION / PURPOSE / ARRANGEMENT

ANALYSIS OF VARIOUS FUNCTIONS OF BUILDINGS

- **DWELLINGS**: SINGLE FAMILY DWELLING, MULTIFAMILY DWELLING, APARTMENT HOUSE, HOTEL, CLUB, RESORT, DORMITORY, INSTITUTION, ETC.
- **COMMERCIAL BUILDINGS**: STORE, OFFICE, DISPLAY SPACE, BANK, RESTAURANT, WAREHOUSE, ETC.
- **INDUSTRIAL BUILDINGS**: LIGHT MANUFACTURING, HEAVY INDUSTRY, ASSEMBLY PLANT, ETC.
- **PUBLIC BUILDINGS**: SCHOOL, LIBRARY, CHURCH, THEATRE, MUSEUM, AUDITORIUM, HOSPITAL, TRANSPORTATION BLDG, GOVERNMENT BLDG, ETC.

THEIR ORDERING INTO GROUPS AND UNIFIED COMMUNITIES
ACCORDING TO THE SOCIAL REQUIREMENTS OF: DWELLING, WORK, PUBLIC ADMINISTRATION, RECREATION, CULTURE

AND ACCORDING TO THE TECHNICAL REQUIREMENTS OF: TOPOGRAPHY, KIND OF BUILDING DEVELOPMENT, HYGIENE AND SANITATION, TRANSPORTATION

REORGANIZATION OF EXISTING CITIES
REGIONAL PLANNING

PLANNING and CREATING

DEPENDENCE UPON THE EPOCH
THE MATERIAL STRUCTURE / THE FUNCTIONAL STRUCTURE / THE SPIRITUAL STRUCTURE

AN ANALYSIS OF THE SUPPORTING AND COMPELLING FORCES OF THE TIMES

POSSIBLE PRINCIPLES OF ORDER:
- THE MECHANICAL AS OVEREMPHASIS OF THE MATERIAL AND FUNCTIONAL
- THE IDEALISTIC AS OVEREMPHASIS OF THE IDEAL
- THE ORGANIC AS THE DETERMINING FACTOR FOR THE ESSENTIAL SIGNIFICANCE OF THE PURPOSES AND PROPER PROPORTIONING OF THE VARIOUS PARTS AND FUNCTIONS OF THE WHOLE AND THEIR RELATION TO THE WHOLE

THE ELEMENTS OF ARCHITECTURAL FORM:
WALL AND OPENING / SURFACE AND DEPTH / SPACE AND SOLID / MATERIAL AND COLOR / LIGHT AND SHADOW / LIGHTNESS AND MASSIVENESS

THE STRUCTURE OF ARCHITECTURAL FORM
THE DEPENDENCE OF ARCHITECTONIC STRUCTURE UPON DISTINCT FORMS OF ORGANIZATION AND WORKING METHODS

THE OBLIGATION TO REALIZE THE POTENTIALITIES OF ORGANIC ARCHITECTURE

ARCHITECTURE, PAINTING, AND SCULPTURE AS A CREATIVE UNITY

PROFESSIONAL TRAINING

- ARCHITECTURAL DRAWING — ARCHITECTURAL DRAWING
- FREEHAND DRAWING AND LIFE DRAWING
- STRUCTURAL DESIGN — STRUCTURAL DESIGN
- MECHANICAL EQUIPMENT AND DESIGN
- SPECIFICATIONS ESTIMATING FINANCING LAW SUPERVISION OFFICE PRACTICE

GENERAL THEORY

- MATHEMATICS AND NATURAL SCIENCE
- THE NATURE OF MAN
- THE NATURE OF HUMAN SOCIETY
- ANALYSIS OF TECHNICS
- ANALYSIS OF CULTURE
- CULTURE AS OBLIGATORY TASK

Program for Architectural Education, Illinois Institute of Technology. 1938. Courtesy of Brenner Danforth Rockwell.

Although less apparent in the first year than later, even here Mies instituted a method of learning framed by intense study of opposites: the highly specific and detailed and the highly abstract and general. In the first year students learned to make architectural drawings as well as to begin to use drawings as a means of seeing in life drawing classes. From the precision of the carefully developed, inked line drawing to the looseness of the life drawing, students began to grasp the range of possibilities of expression and precision available to a thoroughly mastered technique. Despite the tradition that the idea is more important than the thing which represents it, Mies wanted his students to discover that without technique they were without ideas. His preferred version of this concept was through the metaphor of language: that the same words and grammar, syntax and diction that allowed us to speak or write a clear prose also permitted one to create poetry. There were many possible sources for Mies to have encountered this idea. Among them are Valery's *Eupalinos*, in which it is asked "...have you not noticed, in walking about this city, that among the buildings with which it is peopled, certain are *mute*, others *speak* and others, finally — and they are the most rare — *sing*?"[40]

Additionally, Frank Lloyd Wright wrote in his *Autobiography* of Victor Hugo's digression in *Notre Dame* "The book will kill the building," in which he argued that prior to the printing press the greatest poets had been architects, but that now poets no longer needed to build. As with Wright, Mies may have seen this as a challenge, while accepting the premise: *Ut architectura poesis*, architecture is like poetry.

As with drawing, where Mies showed students the technical and the lyrical, so too, poetry was the rare product of an absolute mastery of the techniques of language. What began as measured, logical and rational becomes the means by which one transcends reason to create poetry or architecture. In the following years students studied subjects at the edges of the technical and the abstract. In second year they began with the discipline of the brick and explored the means of seeing through the abstraction of visual training. Even here, seeing is approached in a measured and rational manner, in which decisions are made through comparative study, constantly seeking to find a better expression of the particular problem. When the curriculum moved from means to purposes, the paired nature of problems continued. Here there was the discipline of planning the elements of the dwelling: kitchen, bathroom, bedroom, living room, set against the abstraction of the study of three dimensional space, where the proportions, tensions and relations of elements in two dimensions are extended into three, with the new realm of architectural space to be understood.

In the final stage of undergraduate teaching, planning and creating, the technical and the abstract merge in the development of a building. Not only do students solve all the problems of making the building, they are also prepared to consider its significance as the expression of a unified work of art. The student discovers the idea that only with complete technique are they able to deal appropriately with the concepts their abstract thinking has prepared them to consider.

So far, the description has presented what Mies saw as the purpose of the curriculum for the best students. Mies argued that with one out-

standing student a year, he could transform architecture. He believed all students should be exposed to the possibilities of architecture even if they might not achieve them, while it was the school's responsibility to make sure they were capable of doing whatever they attempted with the best use of material, plan and expression. This accounts for his devoting so much time to the precise and the abstract. Many students were satisfied to master the precise. Nonetheless, they would also be aware of the possibilities of the abstract in the hands of a truly gifted architect.

A corollary of Mies's ideas about the learning process is his assumption that one became intellectually engaged only in adulthood. Much, if not most, university education has been predicated on the opposite assumption, that late adolescence is the period in life when people are most intellectually curious. Mies was struck by the idea that late adolescence is a time of fear of the unknown and an interest in mastery and control. Only with adult experience would a person become strong and free enough to tolerate ambiguities, make judgments and develop

Ludwig Mies van der Rohe. 1938. Courtesy of Illinois Institute of Technology.

Ludwig Hilberseimer, I., and John B. Rodgers. 1938. Courtesy of Illinois Institute of Technology.

Ludwig Mies van der Rohe, Fourth Year Studio Critique. 1939. Courtesy of Illinois Institute of Technology.

commitment to particular values on the basis of understanding rather than authority.

Mies further considered what could be taught as opposed to what could be learned. In visual training, or in studying architectural space, the school exercise provided an opportunity to learn about the subject. Those conducting the course talked about the subject and demonstrated with analogies some of the problems and issues to be considered, but were not expected to be able to teach such sensibilities. This is suggested by our habit of speaking of a sense of color or proportion or scale rather than knowledge. On the other hand, it is assumed that certain skills, techniques, concepts and ideas may be taught. Through demonstration, practice, study and effort, one can be taught to draw a line, but not to learn what a line may mean. One can be taught to build a structure but not how to learn what a structure may mean. One can be taught how to analyze a room, but not how to learn the meaning of a room.

Another factor influencing the curriculum is Mies's recognition that students liked to achieve and demonstrate mastery. He organized the curriculum so a student might feel pleased with a careful drawing, model or analysis, in which all the factors were understood and incorporated in the solution. This sense of assurance would be balanced with the continuing lack of ease students encountered in their more abstract problems, where they were not shown the "right" answer, and in fact were regularly told no such answer existed. Once again, the framing method of the curriculum, the opposition of very specific and very abstract topics, allowed the student confidence in achievement coupled with experience of the continuing challenge of the subject.

This approach also benefitted from technical training capable of producing competent professionals, making the education useful for students of ordinary gifts. Only occasionally would students of extraordinary capabilities be able to do truly creative work with such a curriculum. Nonetheless, the abstraction of the most difficult aspects of the curriculum would be able to earn the respect of weaker students and provide open ended challenges to more gifted students.

Mies often referred to the benefits of teaching architecture in an engineering school, but this was more the rhetoric of the logic of a situation than a necessary, crucial or even central element of his curriculum. He invested little time in learning the strengths of IIT's engineering school. He never created a materials, structures or other engineering and

Walter Peterhans. c.1940. Courtesy of Thomas Burleigh.

architecture laboratory to advance the technical state of the disciplines, despite the fact that he expected such technical experts to develop techniques to answer the demands his new ideas proposed. These included problems of warming, cooling and ventilating his buildings. When he made his proposals for buildings at IIT a number of engineers criticized the solar gain that would result from the large areas of glass. Mies made a few inquiries into the possibilities of developing a glass that would not be thermally transparent, but in the end he chose to rely on venetian blinds on the interior and trees for shade on the exterior. He expected the engineers to develop techniques to solve these problems. In his first few years at IIT, Mies taught the fourth year architecture studio, while also working to develop and study the introduction of his entire curriculum. At the outset, he continued the prior curriculum for upper class students. This was less disruptive to the students' education than the sweeping replacement of old methods with new ones in the midst of their studies. This decision also allowed Mies time to study in closer detail the problems he had begun, while preparing the curriculum in New York the previous winter. Now, in actual classroom situations and in later discussions with his colleagues whom he brought to Chicago with him, Peterhans, Hilberseimer and Rodgers, he could assess the applicability of the curriculum and what, if any, modifications ought to be made in actual implementation.

His colleagues offered a useful range of experience against which he tested his thinking. Walter Peterhans was an accomplished artist and had trained in philosophy as well. Ludwig Hilberseimer demonstrated the role of their comprehensive approach, in which courses in city planning assumed both the skills of execution and powers of abstraction that formed the elements of the school. Hilberseimer taught at the Bauhaus prior to Mies's becoming director, and he aided Mies in restructuring the Bauhaus curriculum when Mies took over. John Rodgers, an American who graduated from Princeton before he studied with Mies in Germany, related the abstract ideas of the curriculum he helped Mies prepare the previous winter, with his actual experience in the studios. Overall, Rodgers was responsible for the technical aspects, Peterhans for the abstract, architectural and aesthetic aspects, and Hilberseimer for the cultural role of the program.

Students during this period included those already admitted, those traditionally attracted by its location in Chicago, and a few attracted by Mies. Not until after the war did Mies's presence, coupled with the increasing fame and extent of his work in America, begin to have a significant effect on enrollment.

Possibly in his first studio in the fall of 1938, but certainly in the spring semester of 1939, Mies began a pattern in his teaching that remained until retirement. By giving students the problem of a university campus, the architecture studio became a research laboratory for thinking about the problems he confronted in his practice. As Armour moved toward its merger with Lewis Institute, the possibility of a new campus developed to the point that at least three architectural offices prepared preliminary plans. Plans were prepared by Alfred Alschuler's firm, and by Holabird & Root.

Although many sites were considered, the plans by Alschuler, Holabird & Root and by Mies were united by their assumption of the 33rd Street campus of Armour as the site. Mies began to study the problem in his fourth year studio, considering the issue at a fairly abstract level by selecting a real but flexible site in Chicago's Jackson Park. From the outset, Mies assumed a campus of many, fairly small buildings. Although only three of these plans have been published, several dozen plans were proposed in the studio.[41]

While this work was going ahead in the studio, Mies also took office space near the Art Institute to begin to study his own thinking for the 33rd Street site. For his staff he hired first John Rodgers and then George Danforth, at that time a second year architecture student. Because of the secrecy necessary for the development of the design, Mies was not provided with a programming document in which the actual needs of the school were analyzed and quantified. Nevertheless, he developed a fairly extensive list of needs for the campus, accommodating the needs for classrooms and laboratories of the existing departments, facilities for the allied Armour Research Foundation, support facilities and what were from the beginning the buildings Mies called "representational," the student union and the library/administration building.

From the abstract, imaginary site of the student designs, Mies moved to one driven by functional concerns, followed by one ordered around structure. When Lilly Reich joined him in the summer of 1939, they studied the latter two approaches simultaneously in order to test and understand their ideas. Rodgers and Danforth would make drawings of the ideas, usually based on Mies's sketches. At this point the twenty-four foot module, later used to set the design more firmly into its site, had not

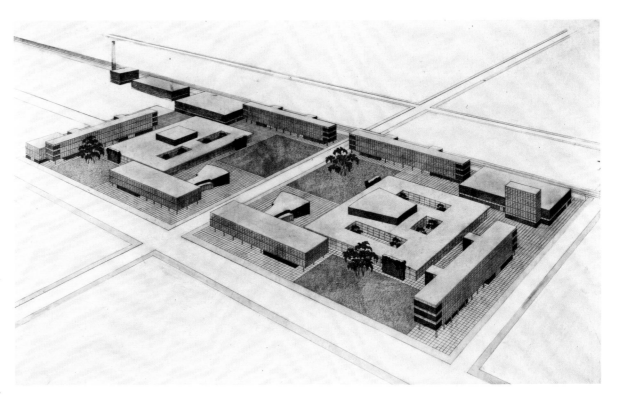

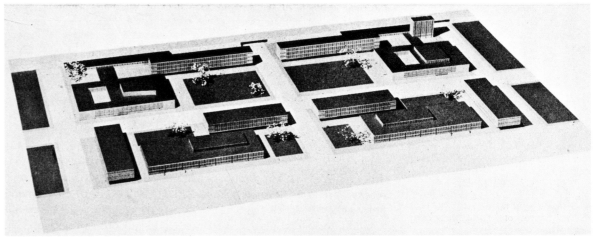

Students Studying Courthouse Problem. c.1946. Courtesy of Illinois Institute of Technology.

Illinois Institute of Technology campus model with l. to r. James C. Peebles, Mies van der Rohe, Henry T. Heald. Courtesy of Illinois Institute of Technology.

Illinois Institute of Technology. Preliminary Scheme. 1939. Courtesy of Museum of Modern Art.

Illinois Institute of Technology. Final Plan. c.1940. Courtesy of Illinois Institute of Technology.

been fixed. In studying what is usually referred to as the Preliminary Plan and what, with modification would be the final plan simultaneously, one can see the same sort of abstract, comparative study and analysis that was emphasized in the curriculum.

More important than the techniques he introduced into the curriculum, with the design of the IIT Campus, Mies completed a major shift in his thinking, consolidating the method that would dominate his American career. This is the use of structure to order the design. Mies's fundamental architectural belief was that his work must incorporate the imperatives of the spirit of the industrial age and give to it an order that expressed the new conditions and provided a vocabulary for future work.

Architecture has long been defined as the successful integration of plan, structure and beauty. In his own work Mies had explored problems of each, but had not determined for himself that any one of the three elements was in some way superior to the others. In many of his works he had achieved a successful solution of two of the elements (form and structure in the Glass Skyscraper Projects and the Barcelona Pavilion, form and plan in the Brick Country House Project and the

Tugendhat House) In the 1930's, with the series of Court House Projects, he incorporated all three elements. Nonetheless, he remained disturbed by the potential for work to seem arbitrary or without sufficient rational and logical power. He desired to achieve something that was not only new and different, but also necessary, unavoidable and correct. This, he believed, gave the new age its special character.

When he began the IIT project, he had determined that form was not sufficiently reasonable to use as the organizing element. In the IIT projects, one, with the auditoriums projecting into the central space, was driven by the idea of the expression of function as the organizing element, while with the other the structure was the central organizing device. While plan and beauty, he believed, were liable to arbitrary, even erratic choices and solutions, structure was clear, easily comprehended and able to order and accommodate the other factors with ease. Structure was a constant inner check which rewarded reason and punished willfulness. In rejecting the plan based solution, Mies called it too "romantic."[42] With the plan founded on structure, Mies advanced his thinking about space, the most intangible and abstract of architectural elements, and structure, the most tangible and presumably most rational of elements, into a position of astringent reciprocity.

As students enrolled at IIT prior to his arrival graduated, Mies completed the transition to his curriculum. During this period he retained the service of some of the earlier faculty, especially Alfred Krehbiel who taught life drawing, Alfred Mell, an architect, and Charles Dornbusch, an architect at Skidmore, Owings, & Merrill, who was interested in modern architecture and, as Mell, had a good rapport with many of the students. As enrollment picked up and Mies was able to teach his curriculum at all levels, he moved Mell from first year to construction and hired one of his earliest graduates, George Danforth, to conduct the first year.

The program was not universally accepted. Heald's files contain a few letters from students or alumni parents which question the wisdom of the new curriculum. Because they were couched in the terms of xenophobic all-Americanism, the value of their criticism of the curriculum is somewhat limited. Already, though, there is the perception that the curriculum expressed a unified point of view so strong that other options were not allowed. Students were not allowed to express themselves or develop their own approaches. The school sought to develop in them a method by which they could study a problem in a deliberate and rational manner through which they could arrive at an appropriate solution. At this point in the development of the program Mies's reputation was not yet so great that his authority pushed criticism aside. Already, the assumption of the curriculum was that the students must first master its ideas before challenging them. Mies and his colleagues were confident in the importance of their ideas and had come to them only after long reflection. They assumed the roles of masters from whom apprentices sought instruction at the rate and amount the teacher deemed correct. Mies rejected the American tradition of the university as a testing ground for the ideas of students. He did not believe that the students could possibly be in a position to doubt and criticize until they had mastered for themselves the logic of the method and system he proposed. The positive result of this would be students of great intellectual and artistic drive and thoroughness, able to solve all the aspects of very complex problems. The negative aspect would be students cowed by the authority of the teachers who would unreflectingly repeat the solutions learned as principles in school.[43] Mies's belief that most of the students would be in the latter position, reinforced his attitude that he should teach sound solutions to those who could not master and transform the principles, while at the same time presenting to the best students an understanding of how the principles of a solution could be abstracted.

As most schools during the war, IIT saw a decline in enrollment and a reduction in the size of the staff because of military service. Mies, Hilberseimer and Peterhans accelerated the curriculum, as teachers throughout the country also did, and found themselves teaching virtually all the courses. They became involved with additional courses designed to enhance the war effort, chief among them instruction in camouflage and aerial reconnaissance. Since the war forced Mies to study the curriculum in an abbreviated form, after the war he accelerated an extension of the curriculum from four to five years. He had learned that the kind of time needed for reflecting on the abstract problems brought about by the expanded and then contracted curriculum was very great and needed to be achieved at a slow pace. One's consideration of alternatives could not be rushed.

The opportunity to expand the curriculum, begun as a study in his first years at IIT, was not reached until after the war. In early 1940 Mies had written all undergraduate architectural school members of the Association of Collegiate Schools of Architecture for their opinion on the five year curriculum. He received the nearly unanimous opinion that the five year curriculum was necessary, and where implemented, was a distinct improvement in the prior four year program. In his letter to the administration on these findings he had concluded

If Armour were to change to a five year program we think the fifth year should be added at the end of the curriculum to give the students further time to develop their abilities by applying the fundamentals, which we feel are pretty well covered in the first three years of the present curriculum, on more advanced problems in Architecture.
We also think courses should be introduced or substituted throughout the curriculum to give the students a broader cultural background than they now possess upon graduation.[44]

When the curriculum was expanded to five years in 1946, Mies's two key points from 1940 were incorporated. Humanities, language, social science and science courses and electives were incorporated into the first four years, while the fifth year devoted 60% of the student's time to architectural studio. Although a formal thesis was never introduced, this great emphasis on the study of one problem provided all students the opportunity to pull together the threads of the curriculum and construct a meaningful fabric. The students knew how to make a building and now could consider what sort of building they ought to make in light of both their architectural method and social philosophy. The final presentation of the problem in terms of model and drawings, finished as well as possible, might be considered equivalent to the journeyman's piece in a traditional master/apprentice structure.

In addition to the development of the five year curriculum, the school began to attract a number of older students, mostly veterans whose education had been interrupted by the war. Their greater seriousness of purpose and desire to form lasting values following the war prepared them to accept the earnest desire of Mies and his colleagues to determine and achieve an architecture for changed conditions. Mies provided students with a sense of belief and purpose after the war in large part because he remembered the sense of drift following World War I. He became for his American students the mentor he had not found in Germany in 1919. He had the further attraction of offering principles rooted in an authentic tradition, while offering solutions based on such principles reflecting the profound changes of the previous decades of war and depression.

Simultaneously, Mies's practice began to expand. At first, he concen-

While the graduate program developed a series of topics for study and exploration, the undergraduate program, in part because of the addition of the fifth year, began to suffer from its success. As the various courses were necessarily less experimental as faculty became more familiar with what would and would not work, they also tended to become more matter of fact, settled and less questioned. Although the virtue and attraction of the school lay not only in its newness, but also in its having a clear point of view, something attractive to students, the faculty were not so critical of their own ideas, seeking to discover means to make the program stronger.

With the rise in enrollment there was a need for new faculty. Among them was A. James Speyer, who in a letter to Mies provides an insight to the attractiveness of the curriculum, while containing a sense of the potential for problems of the future. Writing from Athens, where he was a Fulbright exchange professor, Speyer reported that his Greek colleagues had asked him to remain another year, and asked Mies for his support with the administration:

The school is a good one; it is much better than the French equivalents. Actually, it is based on German educational systems, which because of the *general* relationship to your concepts, may be why I find it more coherent than the schools of Italy and France. Most of the Professors were educated in Germany, and the discipline is strong, and the work hard. The students are like blotters. They are astonished at our way of teaching and criticizing them (I say "our" in the sense of yours, and our way of teaching at Illinois Tech.), and they have shown an eagerness, enthusiasm, and comprehension which is very encouraging. I am chiefly preoccupied with the 4th and 5th year students, a course which takes the same area as mine and Dan Brenner's at home, and I have almost carte blanche to develop the course now. The faculty are very cooperative.

I see, however, and there is no question in my mind at all, that there is no comparison between a school where there are lacks in coordination of the parts, and a school which is completely unified in idea such as ours. (I certainly do not say this as flattery; it is absolutely clear. I have known it for a long time, but the confirmation is always good).

What the students (*and* the architects) here need is an idea of what today's architecture should be, fundamentally. The structural base of form is a thought by no means understood. "Modern" architecture, here as most places, swims along in terms of surface treatment, and it is exciting to see how the students react to an emphasis on the structural derivation of architecture. Amazingly, it is a new thing for them.[45]

Daniel Brenner, to whom Speyer had referred, was one of Mies's most distinguished students, best known for the very beautiful collage of a

Fifth year class with instructors Daniel Brenner (left foreground) and A. James Speyer (at Brenner's left). 1949. Courtesy of L. J. Harrison.

trated on the new main campus buildings at IIT, while also beginning to study a number of projects. Soon, though, his practice, especially through the developer Herbert Greenwald, grew. As the interest of this work spread and the difficulty of building the IIT campus increased, Mies spent less time at school. He taught only in the graduate program. As his practice, fame and reputation increased, he was increasingly viewed as unapproachable. Some of his colleagues at IIT began to protect him from students and as a result he became detached from the day to day life of the school.

With the graduate students, many of whom were fairly sophisticated and had been attracted by the opportunity to study with Mies, there was the opportunity to study problems in depth and complexity. Problems of space, structure, scale and the expression of material were frequently addressed. In addition, many graduate students developed these architectural studies in the context of analyzing a social problem as well. At first these were frequently complexes of many buildings, such as a university campus, or relevant problems, such as the nature of the church in modern times. The question of value was implicit even in studies of the effect of scale, while explicit in such studies as that for the modern church.

concert hall in Albert Kahn's Martin Aircraft Factory. When he joined the faculty at IIT, he taught the architecture studios in fourth and fifth year. In these courses he conducted studies of space, as well as the integration of the fundamentals taught in the first three years, merged with the abstract problems also studied in those years, into the exploration of the solution to actual building problems.

George Danforth rejoined the faculty in this period. Teaching in all the years of the curriculum, Mies prepared him to direct a school of architecture by making sure that he had experience of the character of each of the years of the program.

Also joining the faculty during the post war years was Alfred Caldwell, a person who was to emerge as a force in the school equivalent to Mies and Hilberseimer. Caldwell had entered the school to take a degree in city planning under Hilberseimer. His thesis, "The City in the Landscape: a Preface for Planning," had impressed Hilberseimer tremendously and a place on the faculty followed. Caldwell integrated the two ends of the spectrum. He insisted on great technical proficiency and attention to detail in his courses in materials and construction, and he emphasized the broad cultural impact of architecture in his course in Architectural History, in which the importance of the ethical basis of action and the assumption of the inevitable tragedy of the misunderstood romantic genius were merged. The heroic courage of the architect willing to act despite clear evidence of his necessary defeat tinged all of Caldwell's lectures. Peterhans also offered lectures in history, remarking to students who asked about the difference between his and Caldwell's approach, that his students would understand what he had been discussing in the future. Where Peterhans sought to discern the processes of history so that students could then have comprehension and possible affect on its future course, Caldwell assumed a more mythic structure in which the individual was necessarily opposed to the inevitable destructive forces of time.

When Mies had first developed his plans for IIT he did not give special treatment to the plans for the architecture building. It occupied a position at the periphery of the main plan as part of the ensemble that framed the major buildings on the academic campus, the library and administration building and the student union. In the late 1940's it became increasingly difficult to undertake these buildings and Mies began to think about the architecture building in representational terms. It came to be not only the place where students would study architecture,

Alfred Caldwell with class in S. R. Crown Hall. c.1956. Courtesy of Illinois Institute of Technology.

it became an illustration of his belief in the necessity to study architecture as an extremely meaningful activity. At the dedication of this building, Mies had a gold key made to give to the President of IIT, John Rettaliata. In his remarks at that occasion he said,

But gold is not only bright. It has other more hidden qualities. I am thinking of its purity and its durability. Properties which very well could symbolize the character of the work which we hope will be performed in this building.
Let this building be the home of ideas and adventures. Real ideas. Ideas based on reason. Ideas about facts.
Then the building will be of great service to our students and in the end a real contribution to our civilization.
We know that will not be easy. Noble things are never easy. Experience teaches us that they are as difficult as they are rare.[46]

Since Mies designed S. R. Crown Hall in the time when his retirement from active teaching approached, it should be seen that the building was in part the curriculum raised to three dimensions. The building is a one room school house, in which the students are encouraged and expected to observe the lessons of the other classes. Thus a first year student might see the importance of line weight to expressing ideas in a very abstract study in a fourth year studio, while a fifth year student

Walter Peterhans. 1949. Courtesy of L. J. Harrison.

might see again the necessity of seeing clearly in a second year visual training exercise being considered publicly. In addition to the school's role of presenting to the students the steps and ideas of the curriculum, the physical openness of S. R. Crown Hall served also to invite the public in to see the work. The claims of the school and its curriculum to rationality and applicability to the problems of modern society required that it present its ideas to the public so that they might be assessed. In addition to the abstract nature of the building's teaching the point of view of the school, there was also the demonstration by the building itself of what architecture might achieve. The parts of the building are very clear. One may study the window frames and see the manner and the reasons for assembling their elements as they are. One may study the glass and understand the wide spectrum of expressive possibilities so seemingly clear a material might have. One may study the space, noting its quality and definition and then study its relation to the space of the surrounding campus. One may study its light and see the ways in which the glass itself transforms the membrane that defines inside from outside and gives each an appropriate expression. When the setting or rising sun transforms the space into a reliquary of tinted light, or when the building in darkness is a glowing vessel of artificial light, students and passersby experience the language of architecture as epic poetry. What the student sees is a demonstration of the range of the curriculum, illustrated by one of Mies's favorite aphorisms that "Architecture begins when two bricks are brought together, carefully." That these two poles of the architectural search were important are suggested by two lines of Baudelaire that Mies noted in a letter, after having used them in conversation:

Construction, the framework, so to speak, is the surest guarantee of the mysterious life of the works of the mind.
Everything that is beautiful and noble is the result of reason and calculation.[47]

Mies expressed this concept in another manner when he gave a talk to students at IIT in the mid 1950's on the design of the campus. He concluded his remarks by arguing that the campus,

. . . is radical and conservative at once. It is radical in accepting the driving and sustaining forces of our time . . . . As it is not only concerned with a purpose but also with a meaning, as it is not only concerned with a function but also with an expression. It is conservative as it is based on the eternal laws of architecture: ORDER, SPACE and PROPORTION.[48]

In the 1950's two external events dramatically affected the school. In 1950, IIT merged with the Institute of Design. ID was the heir of the Gropius Bauhaus. Founded in Chicago as The New Bauhaus by a Gropius protégé, László Moholy Nagy, in 1937, it changed its name to the Institute of Design in 1938. The school struggled until after the war when its enrollment expanded dramatically. Following Moholy's death in 1946, the school then secured as its director Serge Chermayeff, who negotiated the merger of ID with IIT. Mies and his faculty unsuccessfully opposed the merger and Chermayeff. ID was administratively a department in the College of Liberal Arts at IIT, just as Mies's school was the Architecture Department in the College of Engineering.

In the early 1950's, however, it was proposed that ID and the Architecture Department be joined in a separate College of Architecture and Design. While this made sense to the administration at IIT, the fundamental difference in attitude between ID and Mies's curriculum was not understood by them, or if understood, thought to be inconsequential. Both Chermayeff at ID and faculty in the architecture department reported their inability to make clear the philosophical differences of the two programs to the central administration.

As their proposal for the Dean of such a merged college, Walter Gropius, who was an advisor to the ID from the time of Moholy until his death, and Chermayeff proposed two individuals, both trained under Gropius at the Harvard Graduate School of Design, Leonard Currie, later a professor of architecture at the University of Illinois in Chicago, and Paul Rudolph, later the Dean at the Yale School of Architecture. For their part, the architecture faculty proposed two alternatives. At the outset, it was clear that Mies was not himself in a position to be Dean. However, he wished to remain as Director of the Architecture program. If this were followed, and there were to be a separate Dean, the architecture faculty recommended Walter Peterhans, one of their colleagues, to be Dean. As a photographer who had himself taught at the Bauhaus, it was argued that he could successfully bridge the differences between the two programs. If it was desired by the administration to have a combined Dean of the college and Director of the Architecture Department, the faculty then recommended that George Danforth, then head of the architecture program at Western Reserve University in Cleveland, be recalled.

The need for Mies's successor had been considered at least from the early 1950's, for he was 65 in 1951, his arthritis became increasingly severe in the decade and his professional practice continued to grow. Mies did not take a leading hand in finding his successor, probably because he did not wish to shape too much the choices of that person. In 1953 Mies had said of Walter Gropius on the occasion of his 70th birthday, that,

The Bauhaus was not an institution with a clear program — it was an idea . . . The fact that it was an idea, I think, is the cause of this enormous influence the Bauhaus had on any progressive school around the globe. You cannot do that with organization, you cannot do that with propaganda. Only an idea spreads so far.[49]

While Mies believed that a school was even better if there were both a clear program and clear ideas, and that it was hard to have one without the other, still he recognized the importance of the idea. Later in the decade, when he had retired from IIT, he wrote in response to a query on how to establish a good school of architecture,

. . . you must first know what kind of school you want. This decision in itself will *determine the quality* of your school. Your faculty should be as good as possible to put over this direction, but the finest group of talented men pushing in the wrong direction or in *different directions* means not only nothing, but chaos. Most architectural schools today are suffering from this lack of direction — not from a lack of enthusiasm, nor from the lack of talent.

If we could only show the schools and faculties that individuality is inevitable and that it, too, has its natural place. To try to express individuality in architecture is a complete misunderstanding of the problem, and today most of our schools either intentionally or unintentionally let their students leave with the idea that to do a good building means a different building, and they are not different — they are just bad.

I believe that in buildings you must deal with construction directly. You must, therefore, understand construction. When you refine this structure and when it becomes an expression of the essence of our time, it will then and only then become architecture. Every building has its position in a strata — every building is not a cathedral. These are facts which should be understood and taught. It takes discipline to restrain one's self. I have many times thought this or that would be a wonderful idea, only to overrule this impulse by a method of working and thinking. If our schools could get to the root of the problem and develop within the student a clear method of working, we would have then given him a worthwhile five years.

Five years is a very short time when you remember that in most cases these are the most formative years to the architect. At least two things should have been accomplished: Mastery of the tools of his profession, and development of a clear direction. Now it is quite impossible to accomplish the latter when the school itself is not clear.

You have, in fact, two possibilities: (1) To set up a school curriculum and find a man who would best carry this out, or (2) find a man who has a clear idea and let him have a free hand in setting the curriculum up in the school. I have never seen the first idea really work out as a strong school. The second idea has worked several times.[50]

Following Mies's retirement, the school was directed by George Danforth. After his tenure, the College of Architecture, Planning and Design was formally implemented in 1975, with James Freed as Dean. Institutionalizing an idea is difficult, and the success at IIT has been mixed. Many factors contributed to the difficulty: personal as well as institutional. Yet these difficulties are not appreciably different from similar problems in any academic bureaucracy. For a time these were overcome by the power of the initial thinking of Mies and his colleagues. However, as Mies had, they too left. Peterhans died during a trip to Germany in 1960, and Hilberseimer retired from teaching in 1967.

When the founding generation was replaced by its students, there emerged the problem of maintaining the excitement of the initial exploration while respecting the importance of their insights. The problem for the school was to honor the form and keep vigorous the idea. The danger appeared in the belief that the form might be so clear that the idea was self evidently implicit. The difficulty for the faculty who taught after Mies is that they had learned what they had been taught, but they had not taught themselves how to learn.

It has been well known that Mies read widely in philosophy, religion and the sciences. In speaking to students once he described the process by which he came to hold his belief in the power of reason:

Little by little one thought is put to another. One is doubtful of a thousand things in this process but by experience and logic you may build upon these thoughts, until you achieve a real conviction and in the end you have such a strong conviction that no one or anything in the world could change it. That is the way it has to be. I don't know if I told you about the time I had 3,000 books in Germany. I spent a fortune to buy these books and I spent a fortune to read them. I brought 300 books with me to America and I can now send 270 books back and I would lose nothing. But I would not have these 30 left if I would not have read the 3,000.[51]

Among the reasons he gave his personal library to the University of Illinois, Chicago, was to prevent his successors the ready access the IIT library might have provided to the 300 books Mies brought to America and the equal number he acquired here. The selection of 3000 books which one might, in a lifetime, winnow to 30, must be identified by the individual, not determined by someone else. Just as the curriculum sought to teach what could be taught and point to what one should consider learning, Mies assumed that his successors would do their own exploring. Yet the strength of his own convictions, and the persuasiveness of his reasoned conclusions, have made it difficult for them to determine the means by which they can direct the school. Clearly the legacy is very great, but its weight of authority is also a burden which many are unable to carry.

In 1949, at the request of Nikolaus Pevsner, who was editing a special issue of *The Architectural Review* on architectural education, Mies wrote:

An architectural curriculum is a means of training and education. It is not an end in itself, but depends on and serves a philosophy. The absence of a philosophy is not a virtue. It is a weakness. A curriculum without a philosophy is not broad and wide, not even neutral, but nebulous.

At the Illinois Institute of Technology we are concerned, among other things, with the idea of structure, structure as an architectural concept. We do not design buildings, we construct them, develop them. We are for this reason concerned with the right use of materials, clear construction, and its proper expression.

Since a building is a work to be done and not a notion to be understood, we believe that a method of work, a way of doing, should be the essence of architectural education.[52]

Implicit in this assertion of the need for clear philosophical thinking is Mies's belief in the appropriate. Whether in terms of material, scale, proportion or expression, Mies constantly sought to teach the importance of understanding the relation of the various elements of either a building or the building's place in the community.

In recent years, as his successors struggle to understand and teach the curriculum in a changed environment, there has emerged the problem of distinguishing the principle and the solution. When Mies taught, this analysis proposes, his general principle was perfectly matched by the actual solution to the problem: material, technique, expression and idea were all located at the leading edge of architecture. Today, when the general principles are advanced in studio, they are illustrated with the same solutions of two generations ago. Such solutions are no longer at the leading edge, and that distance then calls into question the validity of the principle itself. Rather than faculty challenging the students, students now challenge the faculty. Despite the acknowledgement that what he would do was often a surprise, many faculty continue to

consider what Mies would have done today. When the school determines the means to solve this problem, it may be able to reclaim its place at the pinnacle of architectural thought. It has been the site of a great and influential revolution in architectural education, thought and practice. Now it must learn the lessons it has taught so well, to teach them to new generations of students, architects and society.

NOTES

1 Burton Buchhauser to Henry Heald, 12 July 1935, Heald Papers, IIT Archives. (IIT).
2 Willard Hotchkiss to John Holabird, 10 January 1936, Heald Papers, IIT.
3 Henry Heald, Memo for Advisory Committee for Department of Architecture, nd, Heald Papers, IIT.
4 Paul Cret at the University of Pennsylvania, Ralph Walker and Ely Jacques Kahn in New York, William Ralph Emerson at Massachusetts Institute of Technology and Carroll Meeks at Columbia.
5 Minutes of the Advisory Committee for Department of Architecture, Armour Institute of Technology, meeting of 12 February 1936, IIT Archives. Richard Neutra, Charles Dornbusch, Noel Flint, Donald Nelson, Louis Skidmore, Harry Bieg, Percival Goodman, Wallace Harrison, James Mackenzie, Otto Teegan, Henry Richardson Shepley, Shephard Vogelgesang, Arthur Deam, and John Howard Raferty were the young men listed.
6 John Holabird to Mies van der Rohe, 20 March 1936, Mies Archive, Library of Congress, (LC).
7 On the same day, 12 May 1936, Earl Reed had reported to Dean Heald on his recent attendance at the Association of Collegiate Schools of Architecture meeting in Richmond, Virginia. Attempting to make clear his attitudes, he recorded making "many discreet inquiries regarding possible schemes of reorganization of our Department and found everyone, in view of the disastrous Columbia experience, exceedingly shy of a Swedish or German connection . . ." following shortly that "On the other hand you are well aware how easy it would be to secure the Illinois man . . ." meaning Arthur Deam. Reed to Heald, Heald Papers, IIT.
8 Rona Roob, "1936: The Museum Selects an Architect, Excerpts from the Barr Papers of The Museum of Modern Art," *Archives of American Art Journal*, Vol 23, 21, 1983, pp. 22–30.
9 Mies van der Rohe to Willard Hotchkiss, 20 June 1936, Hotchkiss Papers, Architecture, IIT.
10 Mies van der Rohe to John Holabird, 22 June 1936, Hotchkiss Papers, Architecture, IIT.
11 Henry Heald to Willard Hotchkiss, 26 June 1936, Hotchkiss Papers, Architecture, IIT.
12 Charles Butler, Wallace K. Harrison, William F. Lamb, Ralph Walker, and C. Grant LaFarge, chairman, "The Architects' Committee reports on Columbia's School of Architecture," *Architectural Forum*, February 1935.
13 "Columbia Changes Her Methods," *Architectural Forum*, February 1935.
14 Willard Hotchkiss to Mies van der Rohe, 2 July 1936, Hotchkiss Papers, Architecture, IIT.
15 Mies van der Rohe to Willard Hotchkiss, 2 September 1936, Hotchkiss Papers, Architecture, IIT.
16 Alfred Barr to Mies van der Rohe, 19 July 1936, Mies Archive, LC. [Apparently, a copy of this letter does not survive in the Barr papers of the Archives of American Art, for it is not mentioned in the Rona Roob's article].
17 Joseph Hudnut to Mies, 3 September 1936, Mies Archive, LC.
18 Mies to Hudnut, 15 September 1936, Mies Archive, Museum of Modern Art (MoMA), also quoted in Schulze, p. 207.
19 Hudnut to Mies, 28 September 1936, Mies Archive, LC.
20 Hudnut to Mies, 26 October 1936, Mies Archive, LC.
21 Hudnut to Mies, 6 November 1936, Mies Archive, LC.

22 Hudnut to Mies, 16 November 1936, Mies Archive, LC.
23 Hudnut to Alfred Barr, 16 November 1936, Alfred Barr Papers, MoMA, also in microfilm in the Archives of American Art, quoted in Roob, p. 29.
24 Hudnut to Mies, 26 October 1936, Mies Archive, LC.
25 Hotchkiss to Mies, 21 September 1936, Hotchkiss Papers, Architecture, IIT.
26 "Confidential Memorandum, Proposed Appointment of a Professor of Design in the Graduate School of Design, Harvard University." nd, Mies Archive, LC.
27 John Holabird to Hotchkiss, 23 September 1936, Hotchkiss Papers, Architecture, IIT.
28 Holabird to Hotchkiss, 30 October 1936, Hotchkiss Papers, Architecture, IIT.
29 Michael van Beuren to Mies, 3 November 1936, Mies Archive, MoMA, quoted in Schulze, pp. 207–208.
30 Heald to Hotchkiss, 15 September 1937, Heald papers, Dean file, IIT.
31 Schulze, p. 211, reports that Wright himself brought Mies back to Chicago in order personally to show him his work in Racine, Oak Park, Riverside and Hyde Park.
32 Heald to Hotchkiss, 15 September 1937, Heald papers, Dean file, IIT.
33 Mies to Heald, 10 December 1937, Mies Archive, LC.
34 Walter Gropius, *The new architecture and the Bauhaus*, Cambridge, MA: The MIT Press, 1965, esp. pp. 19–44. Gropius wrote this text in 1937.
35 Mies, 1950 speech at IIT.
36 Mies, 1938 speech at Armour.
37 Mies, "Explanation of Educational Program," undated statement, internal evidence suggests [for text, see Appendix] Winter 1937–1938 Mies Archive, LC.
38 Robert Maynard Hutchins, *No Friendly Voice*, Chicago: University of Chicago Press, 1936.
39 Paul Valery, 1871–1945, *Eupalinos; ou, l'architecte*, Paris: Gallimard, 1924; *Eupalinos Oder, Uber Die Architektur*, Leipzig: Insel-Verlag, 1927; and *Eupalinos, or, the Architect*, London: Oxford University Press, 1932. Mies owned a copy of the German edition.
40 Valery, *Eupalinos, or, the Architect*.
41 Johnson, pp. 136–137. The other plans are in the Mies Archive, MoMA.
42 George Danforth, Mies's draftsman at the time, recalls this as the term Mies used to summarize his rejection of this plan.
43 An indication of this attitude is confirmed by the following letter from John B. Rodgers to Linton Grinter, Dean of Armour College, 6 April 1940, Heald Archive, IIT.
   "We are returning herewith the list of books in the library of the Chicago Architectural Sketch Club which you and President Heald gave us ten days ago. Since then we have had our faculty members check over the list. We have had copies of the books which seem to come in question set out for us in the Burnham Library and have gone through them.
   "We are of the opinion that it would not be worth Armour's while to purchase any of these books because they are quite expensive and each such book has only a few plates which would be useful for instruction purposes. It would be far less expensive to have slides of such plates made from the copies of these books in the possession of the Burnham Library."
44 Mies to Linton Grinter, Dean of Armour College, 26 February 1940, Heald Archive, IIT.
45 A. James Speyer to Mies, 28 April 1958, Mies Archive, LC.
46 Mies van der Rohe, Dedication Ceremonies, S. R. Crown Hall, Illinois Institute of Technology, Chicago, Illinois, 30 April 1956, Mies Archive, LC.
47 Mies to Eugenio Batista, 12 March 1959, Mies Archive, LC. [In Mies's own library, now at the University of Illinois, Chicago, there are no titles either of Baudelaire or modern poetry].
48 Mies van der Rohe, notes to a talk given early to mid 1950's, Mies Archive, LC.
49 Mies van der Rohe, [Speech in Honor of Walter Gropius], 18 May 1953, in Sigfried Giedion, *Walter Gropius: Work Teamwork*, New York: Reinhold, 1954, pp. 17–18.
50 Mies to Douglass V. Freret, 8 February 1960, Mies Archive, LC.
51 "6 Students Talk with Mies, February 13, 1952," *Master Builder*, North Carolina State College, Raleigh, School of Design, Student Publication, Volume 2, #3, 1952. pp. 25–26.
52 Mies van der Rohe, [Architectural Education], *The Architectural Review*, 1950.

Items 4–13 lent by Bauhaus Archiv, Berlin.
Items 11 on, if not otherwise indicated, are courtesy of the student.
Asterisk (*) denotes the property of the College of Architecture,
Planning and Design, Illinois Institute of Technology.

WRITING, LECTURING AND BUILDING 1919–1929

During these years Mies addressed the complex issues of modern architecture in order to find a clear expression for them. To do this he made many efforts which showed the problems and their complexities fully resolved. The finished work — strong, uncompromising and assured — suggested that it was the finest possible response to the problem. In similar fashion, his writing and lecturing explored the central issues of the era to find their real meaning and implications. As Mies made his own position clear, in his architectural projects and work, he explored the implications of these ideas for practice. The project for the Brick Country House typifies this effort, showing Mies's interpretation of the material. The project shows great understanding of and fondness for brick, an ancient and handy material. Mies used it to explore the ideas of the new age, without denying its ancient character. In every case Mies showed the difficulty and necessity of simplifying a problem to its essence. This required a careful study of the problem, treating it with the attention it deserved.

1

1.
Ludwig Mies van der Rohe
Two Panels. Glass Skyscraper Study
for the Friedrichstrasse, Berlin. 1921.
Collage.
27″ × 39¼″ (70 × 99.8 cm) each.
Lent by Edward A. Duckett.

2.
"G"
[Zeitschrift fur elementare
Gestaltung]
a. Volume I:
    pub. 1923.,
    2 sheets (photostat).
    17½″ × 22″ (44.5 × 56 cm).
b. Volume II:
    pub. 1923. Original.
    18″ × 11½″ (45.7 x 29.2 cm).
c. Volume III:
    pub. 1924. Original.
    Also Xerox of pgs. 8, 9, 15, 16,
    17, 20, 22, 24.
    10″ × 6¾″ (25.4 x 17.1 cm).
d. Volume IV:
    pub. c. 1924. Original.
    Also Xerox of pgs. 4, 5, 6, 7, 8, 9.
    10″ × 6¾″ (25.4 x 17.1 cm).
Lent by The Art Institute of Chicago.

3.
Ludwig Mies van der Rohe
a. Wolf House, Guben. 1926.
    Photographs.
    Courtesy of Museum of Modern
    Art.
b. Weissenhofsiedlung: Werkbund
    Exposition, Stuttgart. 1927.
    1. Site Plan.
    2. Aerial View.
    Photographs.
    Courtesy of Museum of Modern
    Art.
c. Concrete Office Building, Project.
    1922.
    Photograph.
    Courtesy of Museum of Modern
    Art.
d. Brick Country House, Project.
    1922.
    Photograph.
    Courtesy of Museum of Modern
    Art.
e. Concrete Country House, Project.
    1923.
    Photograph.
    Courtesy of Museum of Modern
    Art.
f. Hermann Lange House, Krefeld.
    1928.
    Photograph.
    Courtesy of Museum of Modern
    Art.
g. Esters House, Krefeld. 1928.
    Photograph.
    Courtesy of Museum of Modern
    Art.
h. Glass Skyscraper, Project. 1922.
    Photograph.
    Courtesy of Museum of Modern
    Art.

2c

2 BAUHAUS AND PRIVATE TEACHING 1930–1937

When Mies became Director of the Bauhaus in 1930 his thoughts about architectural education shifted from informal speculations to practical application. The initial consensus between the school and the local authorities had deteriorated and Mies attempted to stabilize the school by focussing on problems of the curriculum. For his own teaching he conducted an architecture school, making no claims to the universality of such training in relation to other design disciplines. The principle object of study was the dwelling, usually a court house, although variations existed. The problems explored the organization and expression of architectural space. The difficult decisions necessary to express the simplest of ideas dominated the student's time. While forcing students to think in detail and at length of the most abstract of architectural problems, Mies also expected them to demonstrate their ideas in graphically elegant detail. Drawings done for Mies are invariably better than drawings prepared by the same student for other teachers. Mies inherited an existing faculty, including Walter Peterhans and Ludwig Hilberseimer. Through his Berlin colleague, Lilly Reich, he introduced course work in interiors.

Mies's authority derived from his strength of character and, possibly even more, from his status as an architect. This status had been recently confirmed by the critical acclaim accorded the Barcelona Pavilion of 1928–1929 and the Tugendhat House 1928–1930, regarded then as now great masterworks of architecture.

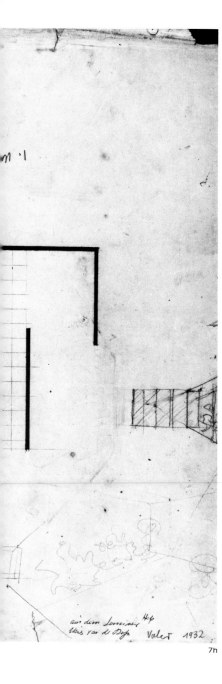

f. For a Ludwig Hilberseimer
   Publication.
   1. Single Family Housing.
      16⅝" × 23⅜" (42.1 × 59.2
      cm).
   2. Two Story Row House.
      16⅝" × 23⅜" (42.1 × 59.2
      cm).
   3. Eleven Story Building with
      Enclosed Corridor.
      16⅝" × 23⅜" (42.1 × 59.2
      cm).
   Ink and colored ink on board.

g. Critique by Ludwig Mies van der
   Rohe. 1932.
   Pencil on paper.
   16⅛" × 20¾" (41 × 52.9 cm).

h. Critique by Ludwig Mies van der
   Rohe. 1932.
   Pencil on paper.
   16⅛" × 20¾" (41 × 52.9 cm).

i. Instructor: unknown.
   Bauhaus, Dessau.
   Regional Site Plan of Group
   Project "Workerhousing for the
   Junkers Works" (with
   C. Vanderlinden). 1932.
   Printed City Map. 1930.
   Various media, mounted on
   board.
   23⅜" × 16⅝" (59.2 × 42.3 cm).

j. Instructor: Ludwig Mies van der
   Rohe
   Apartment House Project. 1932.
   1. Elevation and Floor Plan.
      Ink on board.
      23⅜" × 16½" (59.2 × 42 cm).
   2. Isometric interior study (color
      by H. Scheper).
      Pencil, ink and gouache on
      paper.
      16⅜" × 23¾" (41.6 × 60.3
      cm).

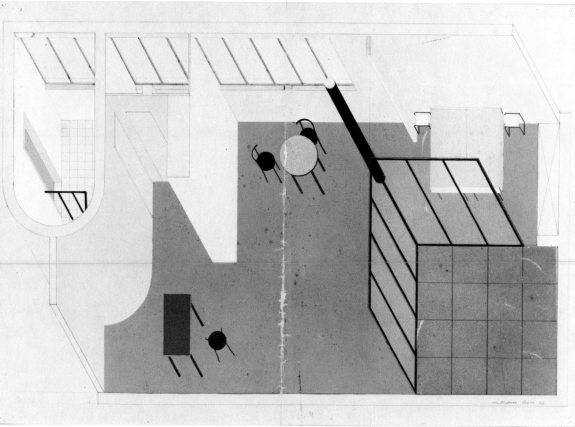

7h

7j2

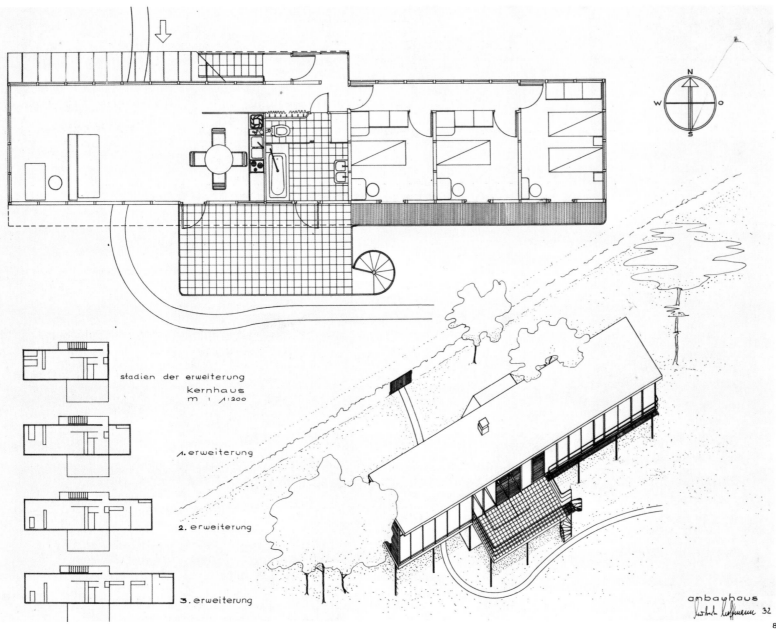

8.
Hubert Hoffman
Expandable House Project. 1932.
Ink on transparent paper.
17⅜″ × 22⅜″ (44.1 × 56.9 cm).

9.
Ludwig Mies van der Rohe
Bauhaus, Berlin.
a. Remodeling of Floor Plan in Factory Building for Bauhaus, Berlin. 1932–33.
b. Remodeling of Second Floor Plan in Factory Building for Bauhaus, Berlin. 1932–33. Location: Siemensstrasse 27, corner Luisenstrasse in Berlin–Steglitz.
Drawing on linen.
12¼″ × 40½″ (31 × 103 cm) each.

stadien der erweiterung
kernhaus
m : 1:200

1. erweiterung

2. erweiterung

3. erweiterung

anbauhaus

10.
Heinrich Neuy
Instructor: Ludwig Mies van der
Rohe
a. Apartment for a Bachelor.
   Floor Plan. Interior Perspective
   and Elevation. 1931–32.
   Ink on paper.
   17″ × 24⅛″ (43.4 × 61.1 cm).
b. Third Exercise.
   Floor Plan. 1931–32.
   Ink on paper.
   17⅛″ × 24⅛″ (43.6 × 61.1 cm).
c. Third Exercise.
   Interior Perspective. 1931–32.
   Ink on paper.
   14¼″ × 24⅛″ (36.2 × 61.1 cm).
d. Fourth Exercise.
   Floor Plan with Corrections.
   Pencil on transparent paper.
   10″ × 18½″ (25.5 × 47 cm).
Instructor: Lilly Reich
e. Room of a Lady.
   Interior Elevation. 1931–32.
   Pencil and watercolor on paper.
   17″ × 24⅛″ (43.4 × 61.1 cm).
f. Grade School.
   Perspective Elevation. 1932.
   Ink on paper.
   17⅛″ × 24″ (43.5 × 60.8 cm).
g. Grade School.
   Floor Plan. 1932.
   Ink on paper.
   17⅛″ × 24″ (43.5 × 60.8 cm).

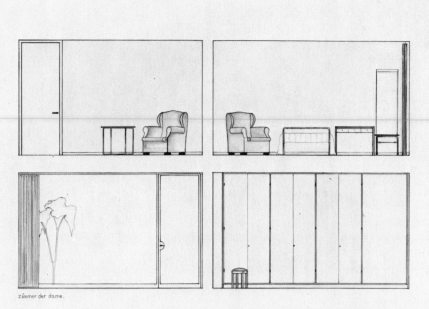

10d

10e

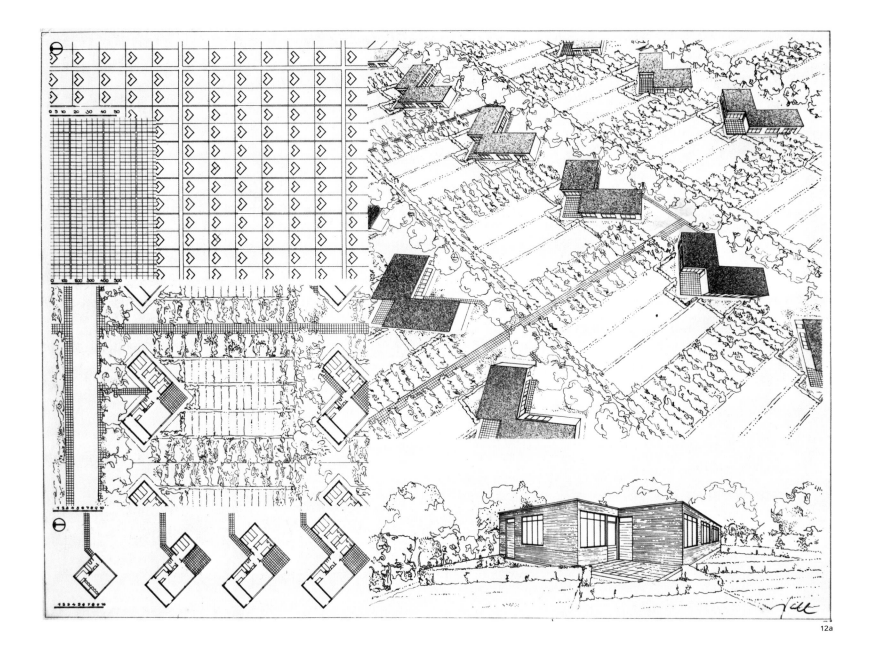

12a

11.
Rudolf Ortner
Summer House Project. 1932.
a. Floor Plan.
b. Interior Entrance.
c. Isometric Interior.
d. Elevation.
Ink, watercolor, collage on paper.
2 — 25⅝" × 19⅝" (65 × 50 cm).
2 — 19⅝" × 25⅝" (50 × 65 cm).

12.
Pius Pahl
a. For Ludwig Hilberseimer
   Das wachsende Haus. 1932.
   Housing Development Project.
   Ink on paper.
   16⅝" × 23⅜" (42.3 × 59.4 cm).
b. For Ludwig Hilberseimer
   Das wachsende Haus. 1932.
   Housing Development Project.
   Ink on paper.
   16⅝" × 23⅜" (42.3 × 59.4 cm).
c. Instructor: Ludwig Mies van der
   Rohe
   Garden View of L-shaped House.
   1931.
   Ink on paper.
d. "Boardinghaus."
   Aerial View. Project. 1930.
   Ink on paper.
   16¾" × 23⅞" (42.6 × 60.7 cm).
e. Instructor: Hinnerk Scheper
   House "C." Color study. 1931–32.
   Pencil, tempera and ink on paper.
   21" × 28¼" (53.5 × 71.7 cm).

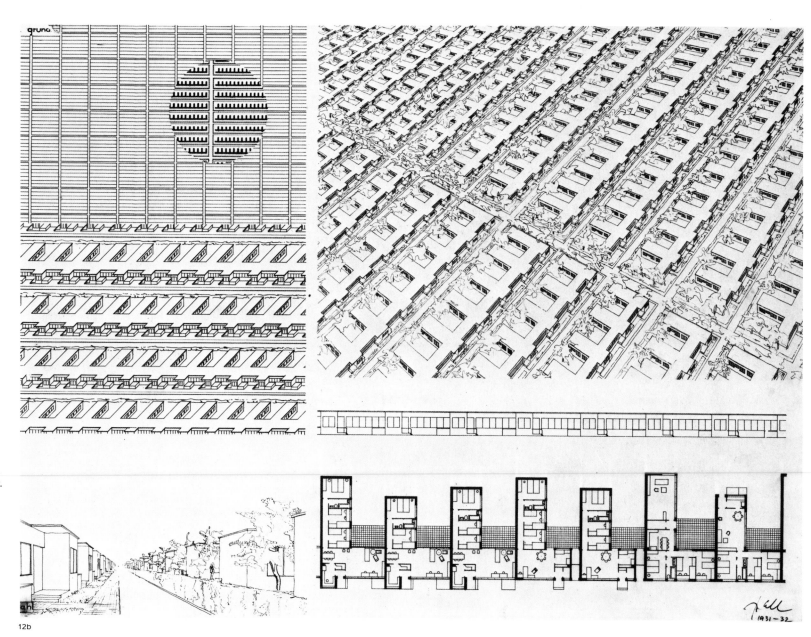

12b

f. Instructor: Ludwig Mies van der
    Rohe
    House "C" Project. 1931–32.
    1. Floor Plan.
        Ink on paper.
        16⅞" × 23⅞" (43 × 60.7 cm).
    2. Entrance Perspective.
        Ink on paper.
        27½" × 39⅛" (70 × 99.5 cm).
    3. Living Room and Bedroom
        Perspective.
        Ink on paper.
        27⅜" × 39⅛"
        (69.7 × 99.5 cm).
    4. Sun Room.
        Perspective View.
        Ink on paper.
        27½" × 39⅜"
        (69.8 × 100 cm).
g. Beach House, Gardersee Project.
    1932–33.
    1. Aerial View from Northwest.
        Ink on paper.
        27⅜" × 38⅝"
        (69.6 × 98.2 cm).
    2. Plans and Elevations.
        Ink on paper.
        27½" × 38¾"
        (69.8 × 98.8 cm).

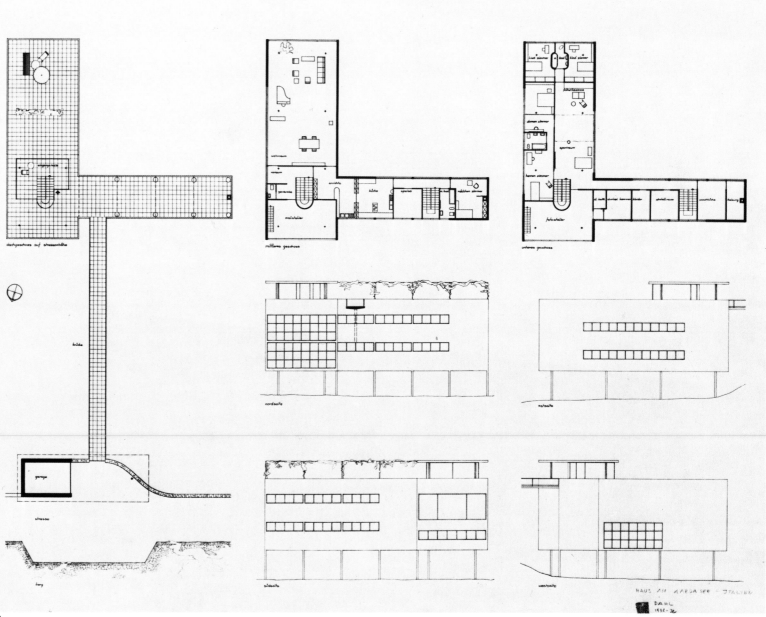

12g2

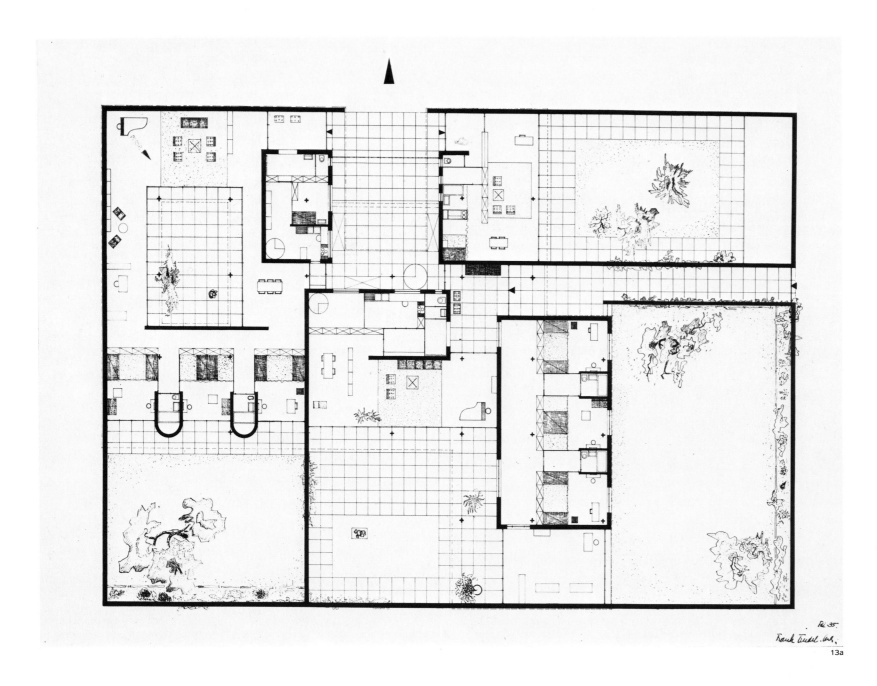

13a

13.
Frank Trudel
Master Class with Ludwig Mies van
der Rohe
Three Court Houses with Common
Kitchen Court Project. February
1935.
a. Plan.
b. Elevation.
Ink on board.
19⅜″ × 27″ (49.3 × 68.5 cm) each.

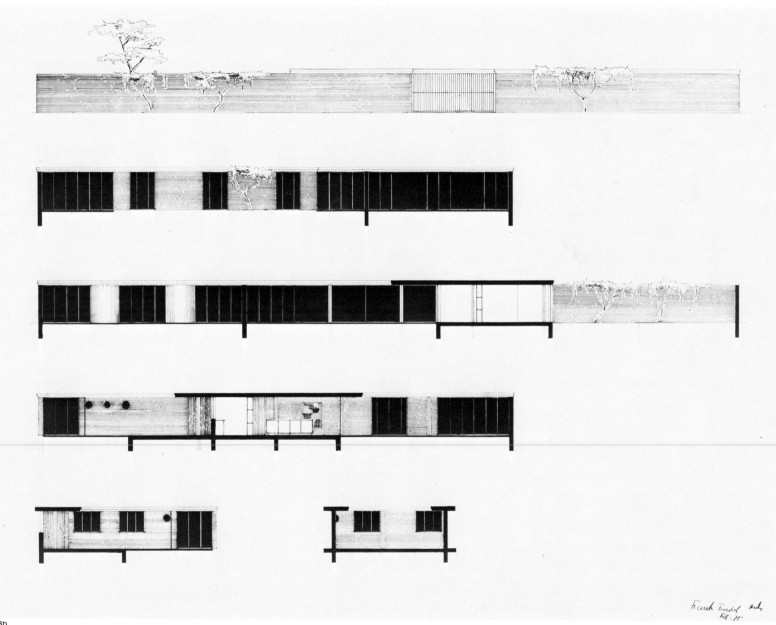

13b

14

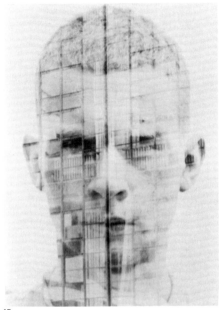

15

17

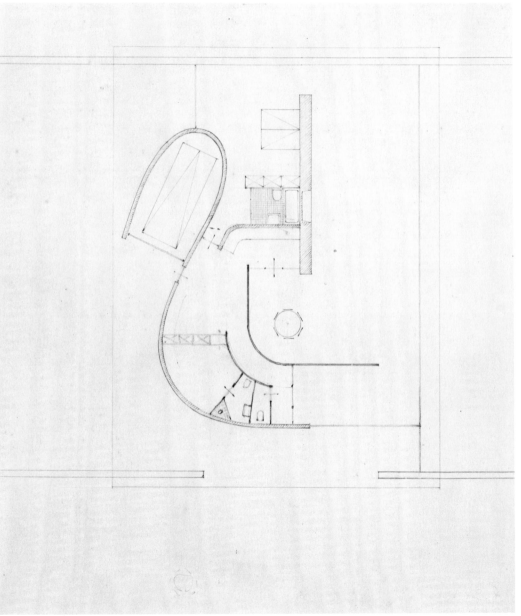

20a

14.
Eugen Batz
Discards with Net and Pieces of
Wood. 1930.
Photograph.
10¼″ × 7¾″ (25.9 × 19.8 cm).
Lent by Rudolf Kicken Galerie,
Cologne.

15.
Hajo Rose
Self Portrait. (Photomontage). 1931.
Photograph.
8½″ × 6¼″ (21.6 × 16 cm).
Lent by Rudolf Kicken Galerie,
Cologne.

16.
Ellen Pitt Auerbach
Sewing Thread. c. 1930.
Photograph.
4″ × 5″ (10.2 × 12.9 cm).
Lent by Rudolf Kicken Galerie,
Cologne.

17.
Grete (Ringl) Stern
Paper in Waterglass. 1931.
Photograph.
6⅜″ × 5⅜″ (16.2 × 13.7 cm).
Lent by Rudolf Kicken Galerie,
Cologne.

18.
Horacio Coppola
Egg and String. 1931.
Photograph.
8⅜″ × 10⅛″ (21.3 × 25.7 cm).
Lent by Rudolf Kicken Galerie,
Cologne.

19.
W. David Feist
Man with Pipe. (Kurt Stulp). 1929.
Photograph.
9⅞″ × 7⅛″ (25.2 × 18.2 cm).
Lent by Rudolf Kicken Galerie,
Cologne.

20.
Michael Van Beuren
Five studies for Court Houses.
1934–35.
Pencil and colored pencil on tracing
paper.
a.   12¾″ × 11½″ (32.4 × 29.2 cm).
b–d. 8¾″ × 11″ (22.2 × 27.9 cm).
e.   8⅝″ × 19¼″ (21.9 × 48.9 cm).
Three studies for Court Houses.
1934–35.
Pencil and colored pencil on tracing
paper.
f.   12¾″ × 29″ (32.4 × 73.7 cm).
g.   11⅝″ × 27⅝″ (29.5 × 72.2 cm).
h.   11⅛″ × 24″ (28.3 × 61 cm).

21.
Ludwig Hilberseimer
a. Mixed Housing Development.
   c. 1920–30.
   Ink on paper.
   13″ × 20⅜″ (33 × 51.5 cm).
   Lent by The Art Institute of
   Chicago.
b. Mixed Housing Development.
   c. 1920–30.
   Perspective rendering.
   Ink on paper.
   14⅜″ × 20″ (36.5 × 51 cm).
   Lent by The Art Institute of
   Chicago.

c. City Planning Proposal, Traffic
   Level. 1925.
   Insert in lower right-hand corner:
   variation introducing three levels
   of traffic.
   Ink on heavy paper.
   23⅜″ × 33″ (59.5 × 83.8 cm).
   Pub.: *Entfaltung einer
   Planungsidee*, p. 17, Ill. 6.
   Lent by The Art Institute of
   Chicago.
d. Central Railroad Station, Berlin.
   Perspective. c. 1927.
   Pencil on heavy paper.
   20½″ × 28¾″ (51.2 × 72.8 cm).
   Pub.: *Entfaltung einer
   Planungsidee*, p. 124, Ill. 102.
   Lent by The Art Institute of
   Chicago.

21b

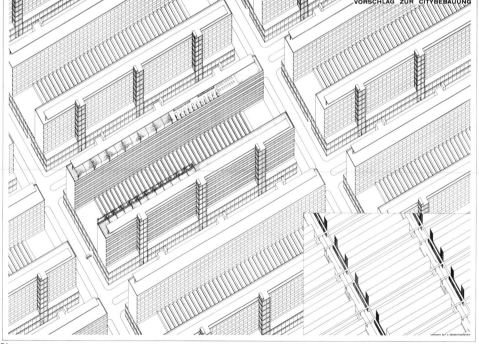

21c

91

26

27

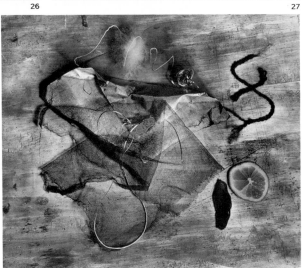

28

22.
Das Kunstblatt
September, 1927.
Paul Westheim, Publisher.
Akademische Verlagsgesellschaft:
Athenaion M.B.H.
Wildpark–Potsdam.
Haus Hilberseimer: Floor Plan,
p. 337.
Ludwig Hilberseimer: Single Family
House, p. 338.
Lent by George Danforth.

23.
Ludwig Hilberseimer
Hallenbauten. 1931.
J. M. Gebhardt's Verlag, Leipzig.
Lent by George Danforth.

24.
Ludwig Hilberseimer
Groszstadt Architektur. 1927.
Verlag Julius Hoffman, Stuttgart.
Lent by George Danforth.

25.
Ludwig Hilberseimer
Internationale Neue Baukunst. 1928.
Verlag Julius Hoffman, Stuttgart.
Lent by George Danforth.

26.
Walter Peterhans
Untitled. Combs & Ping Pong Balls.
Prior to 1938.
Photograph.
15⅜″ × 11⅜″ (39 × 29.9 cm).
Lent by Brigitte Peterhans.

27.
Walter Peterhans
Untitled. Grapes, Lace & Magnifying
Glass on Glass. Prior to 1938.
Photograph.
11½″ × 11⅞″ (29.2 × 30.1 cm).
Lent by John Vinci.

28.
Walter Peterhans
Untitled. Wire and Lemon on Wood.
Prior to 1938.
Photograph.
10⅞″ × 13″ (27.6 × 33 cm).
Lent by George Danforth.

29.
Ludwig Mies van der Rohe
Group of Three Court Houses.
1930's.
Model (reconstructed) by George
Sorich, 1986.

30.
Ludwig Mies van der Rohe
a. Barcelona Pavilion, Barcelona.
   1929.
   Photograph by Berliner
   Bild-Bericht, Berlin.
   Courtesy of Museum of Modern
   Art.

b. Tugendhat House, Brno. 1930.
   View from Garden.
   Photograph.
   Courtesy of Museum of Modern
   Art.

c. House at the Berlin Building
   Exposition. 1931.
   1. Floor Plan.
      Pencil on transparent paper.
   2. Dining Room.
   Photographs.
   Courtesy of Museum of Modern
   Art.

d. Court Houses. 1931–40.
   1. Aerial Perspective View,
      House with Two Courts.
      c. 1934.
      Ink on transparent paper.
   2. Floor Plan, House with Three
      Courts. 1939.
      Studio drawing, pencil on
      drawing board.
   Photographs.
   Courtesy of Museum of Modern
   Art.

e. Gericke House, Berlin–Wannsee.
   1932.
   1. Floor Plan (upper floor).
      Pencil on board.
   2. Floor Plan (main floor).
      Pencil on board.
   Photographs.
   Courtesy of Museum of Modern
   Art.

f. Mountain House, Tyrol. 1934.
   Perspective view.
   Charcoal and pencil on
   transparent paper.
   Photograph.
   Courtesy of Museum of Modern
   Art.

g. Sketch for a Glass House on a
   Hillside. c. 1934.
   Pencil on transparent paper.
   Photograph.
   Courtesy of Museum of Modern
   Art.

h. Hubbe House Project,
   Magdeburg. 1935.
   1. Perspective view of court
      (view from terrace).
   2. Perspective view of terrace
      (view from livingroom).
   3. Model.
   Photographs.
   Courtesy of Museum of Modern
   Art.

i. Ulrich Lange House, Krefeld.
   1935.
   1. Two elevations, preliminary
      version.
   2. Floor plan, preliminary
      version.
   3. Site plan with floor plan, final
      version.
   4. Three elevations, final version.
   Pencil on transparent paper.
   Photographs.
   Courtesy of Museum of Modern
   Art.

j. Administration Building for the
   Silk Industry Project, Krefeld.
   1937.
   1. Main Hall.
      Pencil on transparent paper.
   2. Model.
   Photographs.
   Courtesy of Museum of Modern
   Art.

k. Lemcke House, Berlin. 1932.
   Photograph.
   Courtesy of George Danforth.

l. Reichsbank Project, Berlin. 1933.
   Photograph. Courtesy of Heidrich
   Blessing.

30g

30k

93

3 IIT CURRICULM
1937–1958

In his private teaching after closing the Bauhaus, Mies considered at leisure the problems he had observed in teaching there. When he accepted the appointment in Chicago in the fall of 1937, his thoughts on the curriculum had matured, and he instituted them. Although Mies's curriculum is based on the actual problems of architecture, it is not a version of an office or actual practice. The problems Mies introduced, such as the court house, are simple, clear and highly abstract, and were developed further in the school. Students studied architectural technique to be capable of building simply and clearly. But, the study of technique is also abstract and the lessons learned are in the nature of problems in particular, and problem solving in general.

In bringing Peterhans and Hilberseimer to Chicago, Mies drew on the skills of his former colleagues. Both, however, taught courses that had evolved from their teaching in Europe. While visual training was recognized as a need at the Bauhaus, at IIT Peterhans developed it into a course which taught students visual perception. In America, Hilberseimer's highly abstract analyses in planning characteristic of his European teaching, expanded to include an ecological approach, addressing itself to the particularities of the individual site in addition to the application of general principles.

124c

94

31.
Albert Goers
Archeo Design Problem. c. 1936.
Ink wash on watercolor paper.
38″ × 24⅜″ (96.5 × 62 cm).

32.
Albert Goers
Archeo Design Problem. c. 1936.
Sepia wash and pencil on Watman's
watercolor paper.
22½″ × 29⅛″ (57 × 74 cm).

33.
Albert Goers
Architectural Drawing, 1st Year.
Art Institute Doorway, East Facade
overlooking McKlintock Court.
c. 1934.
Elevation.
Ink wash on watercolor paper.
26⅝″ × 20¾″ (67.5 × 52.5 cm).

34.
Ivar Viehe-Naess, Jr.
Class B — III Project.
An Open Air Museum. c. 1937.
Ink wash on watercolor paper.
39⅝″ × 28⅝″ (100.5 × 72.5 cm).
Lent by Raymond Kliphardt.

35.
Raymond Kliphardt
Class B — Project II.
A Country Restaurant. c. 1937.
Watercolor on watercolor paper.
28″ × 39″ (71 × 99 cm).

36.
Raymond Kliphardt
Class B — Project III.
A Book Store. c. 1937.
Ink wash on watercolor paper.
27¾″ × 38″ (70.5 × 96.5 cm).

36

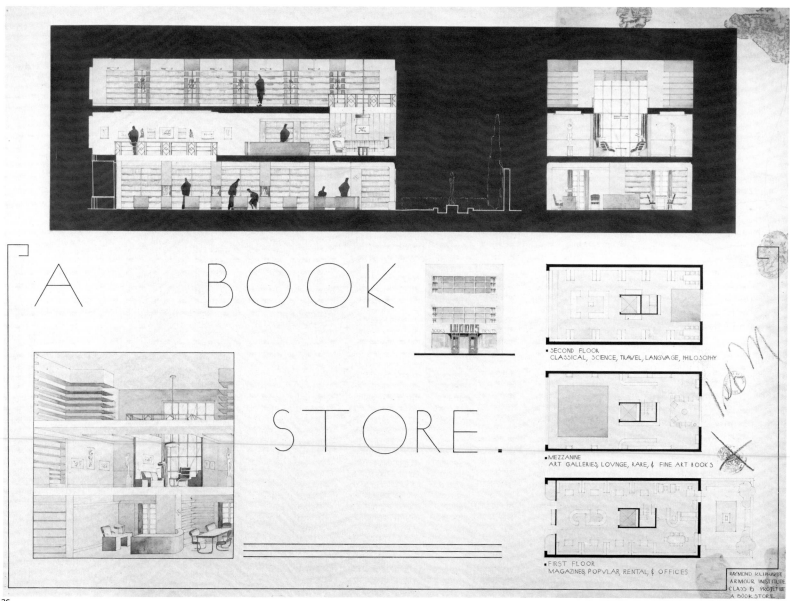

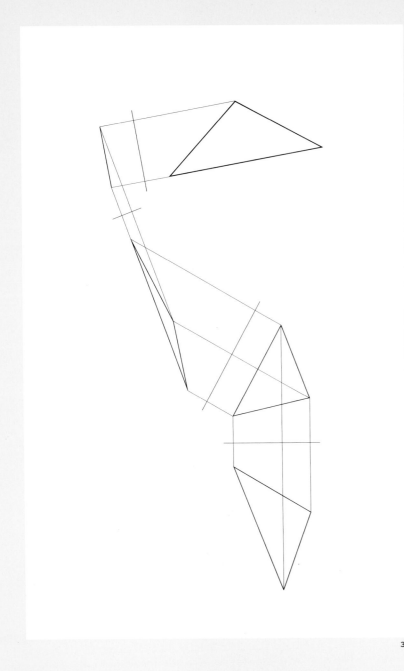

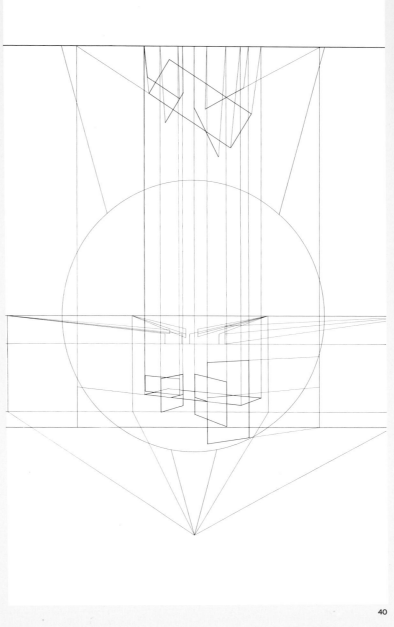

37.
Raymond Kliphardt
Class B — Project IV.
A Cinema Lobby. c. 1936–37.
Watercolor on watercolor paper.
28¾" × 39¼" (73 × 99.5 cm).

38.
R. Smith
Applied Descriptive Geometry 102.
Revolution of Triangular Plane to
Determine True Size and Angles of
Sides. 1950.
Ink on Strathmore board.
30" × 20" (76 × 51 cm).*

39.
Robert Kissinger
Applied Descriptive Geometry 102.
Intersection of Solids. 1950.
Pencil on Strathmore board.
30" × 20" (76 × 51 cm).*

40.
Donald Wrobleski
Perspective 108.
Perspective Projection. c. 1949–50.
Ink on Strathmore board.
30" × 20" (76 × 51 cm).

41.
Richard L. Svec
Applied Descriptive Geometry 104.
Development of an Ellipse. 1951.
Ink on Strathmore board.
30" × 20" (76 × 51 cm).*

42.
Edward Starostovic
Axonometric Projection 103.
Revolution of Line and Plane. Spring
1952.
Ink on Strathmore board.
30" × 20" (76 × 51 cm).

38

40

43.
Anonymous
Applied Descriptive Geometry 104.
Two Lines Intersecting.
Late 1950's.
Ink and colored ink on paper.
29″ × 20″ (73.6 × 51 cm).
Lent by John Vinci.

44.
W. Kosterman
Elementary Drafting 103.
Line Weight Exercise. c. 1961–62.
Ink on paper.
29″ × 20″ (73.6 × 51. cm).*

45.
Vernon Geisel
Elementary Drafting 103.
Line Weight Exercise. 1963.
Pencil on paper.
29″ × 20″ (73.6 × 51 cm).*

46.
Peter Lewis
Elementary Drafting 103.
Exercise with Tangential Circles.
1968–69.
Ink on paper.
29″ × 20″ (73.6 × 51 cm).*

47.
Freeze
Elementary Drafting 103.
Exercise with Tangential Circles.
c. 1963.
Pencil on paper.
29″ × 20″ (73.6 × 51 cm).*

48.
Mary Elizabeth (Droste) Spies
Materials and Construction 207.
Horizontal Log Construction. 1939.
Pencil on Strathmore board.
30″ × 40″ (76 × 101.6 cm).
Lent by R. Ogden Hannaford.

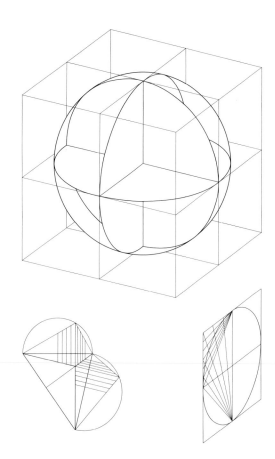

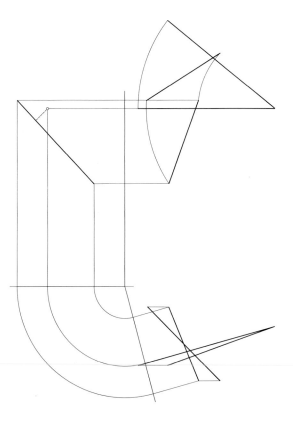

41

42

49.
Richard E. Johnson
Materials and Construction 207, 208.
Brick Bearing Wall House. Cut-Away
Perspective. 1948–49.
Pencil on Strathmore board.
30″ × 40″ (76 × 101.6 cm).*

50.
Anonymous
Materials and Construction 213, 214.
Brick Bonding Exercise. c. 1956–57.
Isometric.
Pencil on Strathmore board.
30″ × 20″ (76 × 51 cm).
Lent by John Vinci.

51.
M. Von Broembsen
Materials and Construction 213, 214.
Brick Courthouse Construction.
1958.
a. Elevations/Sections.
b. Perspective.
Pencil on Strathmore board.
30″ × 40″ (76 × 101.6 cm).
Lent by John Vinci.

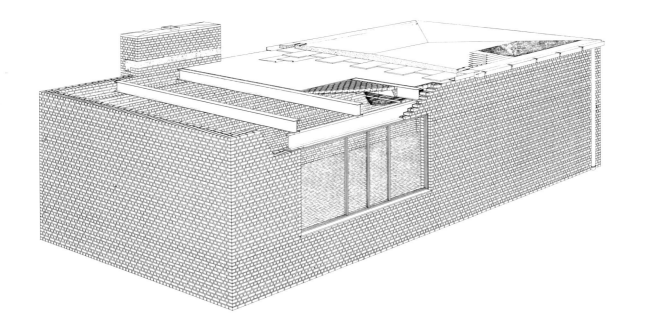

49

52.
Gene Maloney
Materials and Construction 213.
Brick Bearing Wall Construction.
January 1961.
Plan and Section.
Pencil on Strathmore board.
30" × 40" (76 × 101.6 cm).*

53.
David Spaeth
Materials and Construction 214.
Wood Frame House on Stone Base.
3 June 1961.
Perspective.
Pencil on Strathmore board.
30" × 40" (76 × 101.6 cm).*

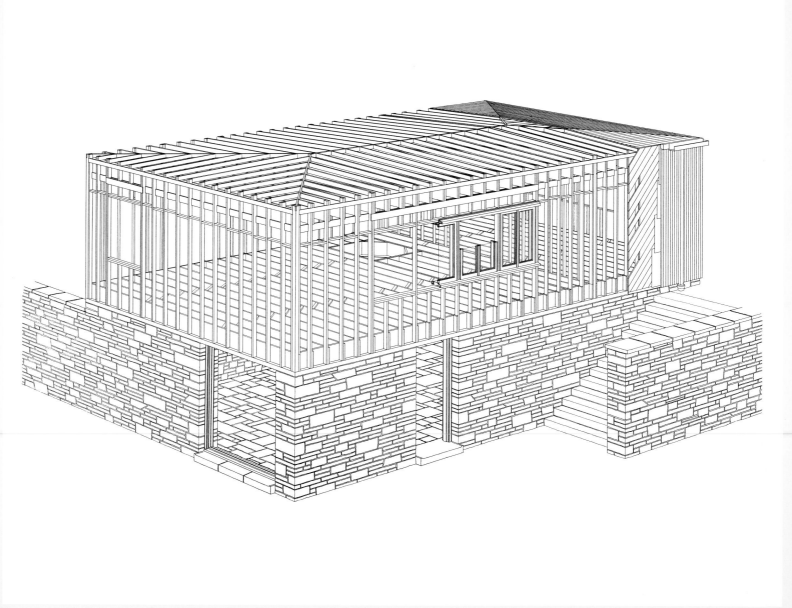

53

54.
Katherine Barr
Materials and Construction 213.
Brick Bearing Wall Construction.
19 January 1967.
Perspective Section.
Pencil on Strathmore board.
30″ × 40″ (76 × 101.6 cm).*

55.
Carter H. Manny, Jr.
Architectural Construction 311.
Courthouse Problem. 1947.
a. Sections.
b. Full Scale Window Details.
c. Perspective.
Pencil on illustration board.
30″ × 40″ (76 × 101.6 cm) each.

55

56.
Edmond N. Zisook
Architectural Construction 311, 312.
Brick Crosswall House. 1948–49.
Perspective.
Pencil on Strathmore board.
30″ × 40″ (76 × 101.6 cm).

56

57.
Donald Wrobleski
Architectural Construction 311, 312.
Brick Bearing Wall with Concrete
Roof Using Elementary School Plan.
1951–52.
Perspective Section.
Pencil on Strathmore board.
30″ × 40″ (76 × 101.6. cm).

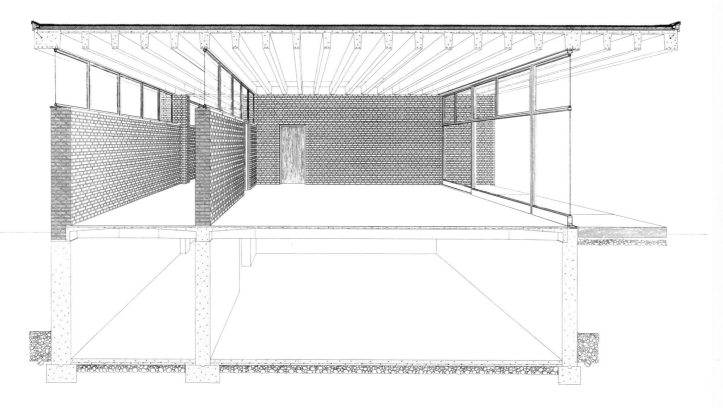

57

58.
Kenneth Folgers
Architectural Construction 311, 312.
Shell Construction Using Elementary
School Plan. 1955–56.
Perspective Section.
Pencil on Strathmore board.
30″ × 40″ (76 × 101.6 cm).

59.
Anonymous
Architectural Construction 311, 312.
Brick Wall and Roof. c. 1957–58.
Full Size Detail.
Pencil and colored pencil on
Strathmore board.
30″ × 40″ (76 × 101.6 cm).
Lent by John Vinci.

60.
Thomas Burleigh
Architecture 407, 408.
Steel Skeleton Highrise Curtain Wall
Study. c. 1942–43.
Pencil and ink on back of blueprint.
39½″ × 30″ (101.3 × 76 cm).

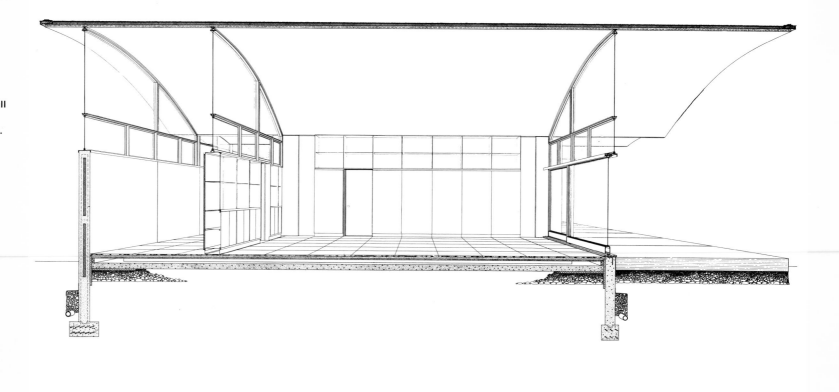

58

61.
Joseph Fujikawa
Architecture 407, 408.
Concrete Skeleton Highrise Curtain
Wall Study. 1944.
Photograph by Hedrich Blessing.

62.
Bruno Conterato
Architecture 408.
Courthouse Problem. 1948.
Interior Perspective.
Collage on Strathmore board.
30″ × 40″ (76 × 101.6 cm).*

63.
Robert Reeves
Architecture 407, 408.
Brick Bearing Wall Bachelor's
House. 1949–50.
Plan and Elevations.
Pencil on Strathmore board.
30″ × 40″ (76 × 101.6 cm).*

64.
Allen Marske
Architecture 404.
Wall Problem with Two Sculptures.
Collage on grey board.
15″ × 20″ (38.1 × 51 cm).*

65.
Walter Romberg
Architecture 404.
Wall Problem with Two Paintings
and a Shelf. c. 1965.
Collage on grey board.
15″ × 20″ (38.1 × 51 cm).*

66.
J. Spacek
Architecture 404.
Wall Problem with Painting and
Sculpture. 1970.
Collage on grey board.
15″ × 20″ (38.1 × 51 cm).*

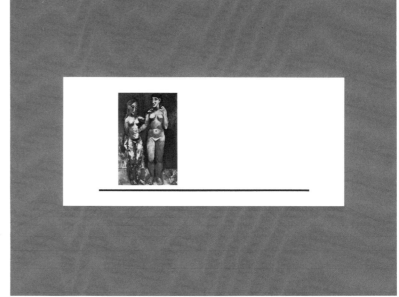

61

67

104

67.
Gil Walendy
Architecture 403.
Wall Problem with Painting and
Shelf. 1968.
Collage on grey board.
15″ × 20″ (38.1 × 51 cm).*

68.
Donald Sickler
Architecture 444.
A Campus Plan. 1953.
Perspective.
Pencil and ink wash on Strathmore
board.
30″ × 40″ (76 × 101.6 cm).*

69.
Anonymous
Architecture 444.
A Campus Plan. 1955–57.
Two Perspectives.
a. Conte pencil on Strathmore
    board.
b. Conte pencil with lipstick on
    Strathmore board.
30″ × 40″ (76 × 101.6 cm) each.*

70.
B. Babka
Architecture 444.
Highrise/Lowrise Waterfront
Development Project. c. 1956.
Site Plan.
Pencil on Strathmore board.
30″ × 40″ (76 × 101.6 cm).*

71.
Marcia (Gray) Martin
Architecture 444.
Highrise/Lowrise Waterfront
Development Project. 1956.
Elevation Study.
Pencil on Strathmore board.
10¼″ × 40″ (26 × 101.6 cm).*

69a

105

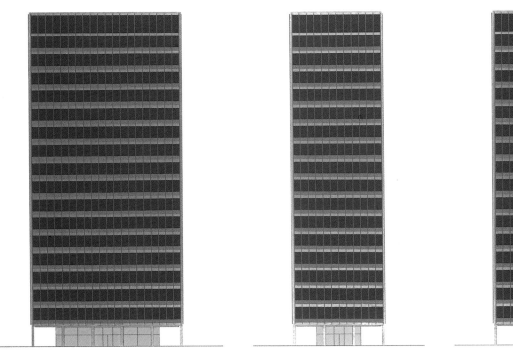

72.
Cynthia (Bostick) Lenz
Architecture 444.
Highrise/Lowrise Waterfront
Development Project. 1956.
Perspective.
Pencil on Strathmore board.
30" × 40" (76 × 101.6 cm).*

73.
R. Linke (Designer)
B. Samuels (Draftsman)
Architecture 444.
Highrise/Lowrise Waterfront
Development Project. 1956.
Site Plan.
Pencil on Strathmore board.
30" × 40" (76 × 101.6 cm).*

74.
G. Osako
Architecture 444.
Highrise/Lowrise Waterfront
Development Project. 1956.
Site Plan.
Pencil on Strathmore board.
10¼" × 40" (26 × 101.6 cm).*

75.
Marilyn Ternovits
Architecture 405, 406.
Highrise. 1 May 1967.
Elevation Studies.
Collage on Strathmore board.
30" × 40" (76 × 101.6 cm).*

76.
Thomas Burleigh
Visual Training 211.
Exercise with Textures. 25 January
1941.
Collage on illustration board.
30" × 20" (76 × 51 cm).

75

77.
H. Seklemian
Visual Training 211, 212.
Exercise in Proportion. c. 1943–44.
Collage on board.
30″ × 20″ (76 × 51 cm).
Lent by the Chicago Historical
Society.

78.
L. Blinderman
Visual Training 211, 212.
Exercise in Proportion. c. 1944–45.
Collage on board.
30″ × 20″ (76 × 51 cm).
Lent by the Chicago Historical
Society.

79.
J. Somers
Visual Training 211, 212.
Exercise in Proportion. c. 1945–46.
Collage on board.
30″ × 20″ (76 × 51 cm).
Lent by the Chicago Historical
Society.

80.
J. Somers
Visual Training 211, 212.
Exercise in Proportion. c. 1945–46.
Collage on board.
30″ × 20″ (76 × 51 cm).
Lent by the Chicago Historical
Society.

81.
David J. Tamminga
Visual Training 212. 1947.
a. Exercise with Textures.
b. Exercise with Textures.
c. Intersecting Planes.
Collage on illustration board.
30″ × 20″ (76 × 51 cm) each.

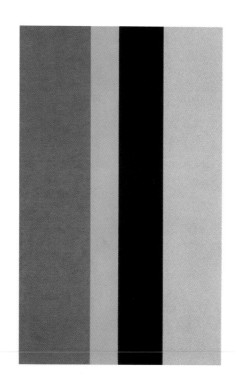

76

81c

107

82.
John Munson
Visual Training 212.
Planes in Space. May 1954.
Collage on illustration board.
30″ × 20″ (76 × 51 cm).

83.
Edward Starostovic
Visual Training 212.
Exercise with Warped Planes.
January 1953.
Pencil on Strathmore board.
30″ × 20″ (76 × 51 cm).

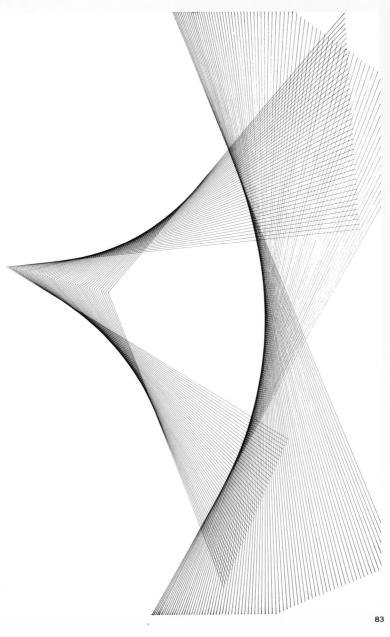

84.
John Vinci
Visual Training 211, 212.
Exercise in Proportion. 1956–57.
Collage on illustration board.
30″ × 20″ (76 × 51 cm).

85.
John Munson
Visual Training 306.
Exercise with Textures. January
1955.
Ink and colored ink on paper.
28⅛″ × 19¾″ (71.5 × 50 cm).
Mounted on illustration board.
30″ × 20″ (76 × 51 cm).

86.
David Sharpe
Visual Training 306.
Exercise with Natural Textures.
1958.
Colored inks on illustration board.
30″ × 20″ (76 × 51 cm).

87.
John Vinci
Visual Training 305, 306.
Exercise with Created Textures.
1957–58.
Ink wash on illustration board.
30″ × 20″ (76 × 51 cm).

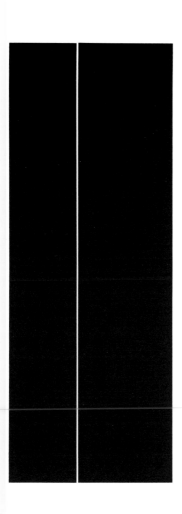

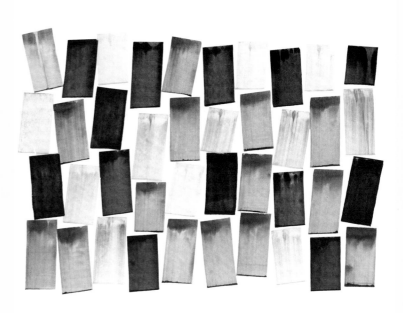

84

85

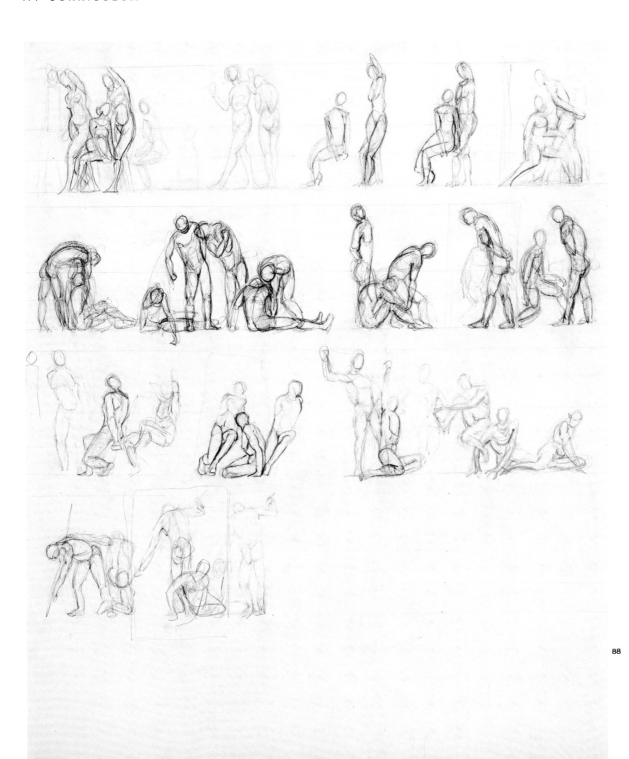

88.
Thomas Burleigh
Freehand Drawing 205.
Figure Studies. 6 November 1940.
Pencil on paper.
24″ × 18″ (61 × 45.5 cm).

89.
Terry Imamuro
Lawrence Kenny
Albert Roupp
Mel Skavarla
Life Drawing.
Four Studies of Plant Life.
c. 1959–60.
Pencil and ink on paper.
11″ × 8½″ (27.8 × 21.5 cm).
Mounted on illustration board.
30″ × 20″ (76 × 51 cm).*

90.
Tolee
Freehand Drawing.
Seated Male Figure.
Ink wash on paper.
23½″ × 17¾″ (59.7 × 45.1 cm).
Mounted on illustration board.
30″ × 20″ (76 × 51 cm).*

91.
Michael Heider
Life Drawing.
Seated Male Figure. 1966–67.
Pencil on paper.
24″ × 17¾″ (61 × 45.1 cm).
Mounted on illustration board.
30″ × 20″ (76 × 51 cm).*

92.
Eric Anderson
City Planning 201.
City Block Density Studies.
22 January 1948.
Ink on Strathmore board.
30″ × 20″ (76 × 51 cm).*

93.
Anonymous
City Planning.
Housing Detail of Settlement Unit.
Ink on illustration board.
30″ × 20″ (76 × 51 cm).*

94.
Anonymous
City Planning.
Housing and Community Buildings,
Sun Pentration Studies.
Ink on Strathmore board.
30″ × 20″ (76 × 51 cm).*

95.
Alfred Caldwell
City Planning.
Density Studies, Comparison of
Building Shapes.
Ink on Strathmore board.
30″ × 20″ (76 × 51 cm).*

96.
Anonymous
City Planning.
Housing and Community Buildings,
Sun Chart.
Ink on Strathmore board.
20″ × 30″ (51 × 76 cm).*

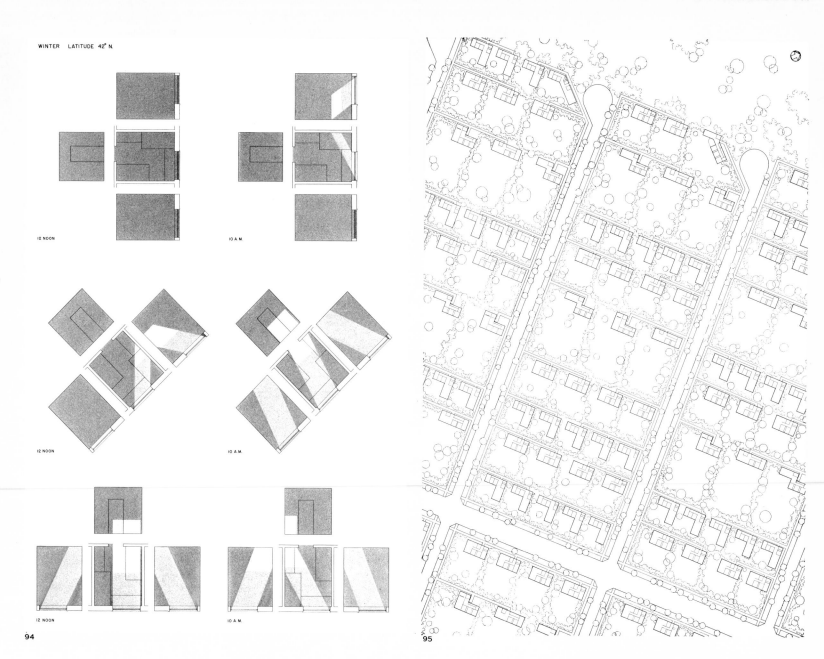

94

95

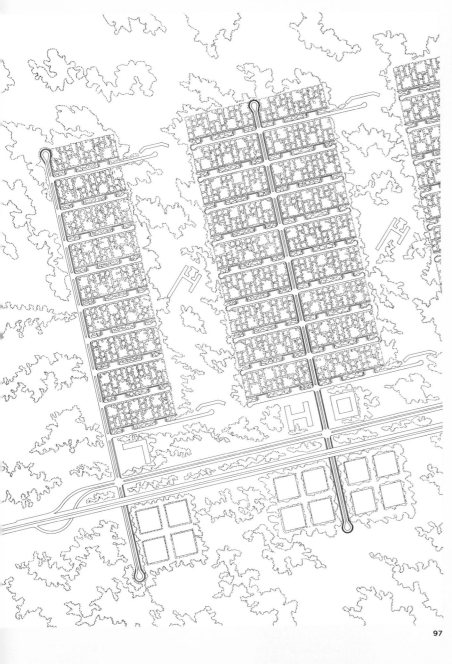

97

97.
C. S. Stanfield
City Planning.
Settlement Unit Project.
Ink on illustration board.
29¾″ × 22½″ (75.7 × 57 cm).*

98.
Anonymous
Regional Planning.
City Along a River.
Ink and wash on Strathmore board.
30″ × 22½″ (76 × 57 cm).*

99.
Shields
Regional Planning.
Rock River Valley. Plan and
Variation.
Ink on Strathmore board.
30″ × 20″ (76 × 51 cm).*

100.
Architectural Construction.
a. Traditional Timber-Framed
    Building. Scale Model: Oak.*
b. Traditional Timber-Framed
    Building. Scale Model: Oak.*
c. Prototype Balloon Frame
    Construction.
    Model: Wood House on Stone
    Walls.
    Basswood and Travertine.
    Scale: ¼″ = 1′-0″.*
d. Steel Skeleton Medium Rise
    Building. Scale Model: Metal.*
e. Long Span Open Truss System,
    200′ × 400′. Model: Metal.
    Scale: 1/16″ = 1′-0″.*

101.
Anonymous
Architecture 453-454.
Model of Building Groupings.
Late 1950's.
Photograph.
Courtesy of George Danforth.

102.
George Danforth
House with Three Courts. c. 1940.
Perspective of Bedroom Wing.
Photograph by Hedrich Blessing.

103.
George Danforth
Architecture 407, 408.
Notebook of Design Sketches with
Critiques by Mies. 1939–40.
Notebook with pencil on tracing
paper.
9″ × 14½″ (23.9 × 36.8 cm).

104.
Thomas Burleigh
Student File with Problems and
Information Handouts Given to
Students. 1947-48.
File.
11¾″ × 9½″ (29.8 x 24.1 cm).

105.
Exhibit in Skylight Space Outside
Architecture Department Offices,
Top of The Art Institute of Chicago.
c. 1941.
Photograph by Thomas Burleigh.

106.
Eight Images of the Open House
Exhibit, Alumni Memorial Hall,
Illinois Institute of Technology.
c. 1947.
Photographer unknown. Courtesy of
George Danforth.

107.
Four Views Open House Exhibit,
Second Floor, Armour Mission,
Armour Institute of Technology.
1942.
Photograph by George Storz.

108.
Ludwig Mies van der Rohe
Five Views of the Mies Exhibit at the
Renaissance Society. 1947.
Photographs by Hedrich Blessing.

109.
Open House Exhibit at Lakeview
Building, Chicago. Model of 10-Story
Apartment House by James
Michaelson and R. Ogden
Hannaford. 1940-41.
Photograph by R. Ogden Hannaford.

110.
Open House Exhibit, Alumni
Memorial Hall, Illinois Institute of
Technology. c. 1948.
a.   City Planning Model.
b.   IIT Campus Model.
c.   Elevations Studies.
d-f. General Views of the Exhibit.
Photographs by Thomas Burleigh.

105

106

107

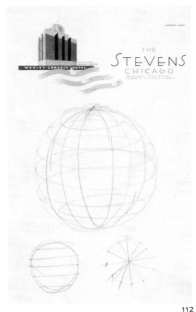

112

112

113

111.
Five Images of Faculty Lecturing at Alumni Memorial Hall, Illinois Institute of Technology. c. 1949.
a-c.   A. James Speyer and Daniel Brenner Holding a Class.
d.   Peterhans at Podium.
e.   Brenner Critiquing Drawings.
Photographs by Lawrence J. Harrison.

112.
Alfred Mell or John Rodgers
Six Sketches of Freshman Drawing Exercises, Working Out the Courses with Mies and Peterhans.
c. 1938–39.
Pencil on hotel stationery.
8½″ × 5½″ (216 × 13.9 cm) each.

113.
Lawrence J. Harrison
Caricature Sketch of A. James Speyer, Faculty of Architecture, Illinois Institute of Technology.
c. 1949.
Pencil on note paper.
5⅞″ × 8 ⅜″ (15 × 21.1 cm).

114.
Hilberseimer Giving a Critique to Students, The Art Institute of Chicago. c. 1941.
Photograph by R. Schneider.
Courtesy of Thomas Burleigh.

115.
Hilberseimer with Students. c. 1955.
Photograph by R. J. Martin.
Lent by Marcia Gray Martin.

116.
Hilberseimer with Junior Students, John Randall and Henry Boles (r.).
c. 1941.
Photograph by Thomas Burleigh.

117.
Two Images of Mies at Hilberseimer's Day Party, Art Institute of Chicago, Corridor.
21 December 1942.
Photograph by Thomas Burleigh.

118.
Mies Giving a Critique to Student, Drafting Room at The Art Institute of Chicago. c. 1941.
Photograph by R. Schneider.
Courtesy of Thomas Burleigh.

119.
Four Images of Hilberseimer's Day in the Loop, Chicago. c. 1941.
Photographer unknown.
Courtesy of Thomas Burleigh.

120.
Image of Hilberseimer, Signed by the Class of 1949 on the Back. c. 1949.
Photographer unknown.
6¾″ × 4¾″ (17.2 x 12.2 cm).

121.
Hilberseimer Giving a Critique to Students. c. 1949.
Photographer unknown.
Courtesy of Lawrence J. Harrison.

122.
Mies at Open House Exhibit, Alumni Memorial Hall, Illinois Institute of Technology. 1949.
Photographer unknown.
Courtesy of Lawrence J. Harrison.

123.
Mies in S. R. Crown Hall, Illinois Institute of Technology. Mid-1950's.
Photograph by Hedrich Blessing.

124.
Ludwig Mies van der Rohe
a. Resor House. Second Scheme. Model. c. 1938.
    Photograph by Hedrich Blessing.
b. Hi-Way Restaurant Project, Indianapolis. Model. 1946.
    1. Photograph by Hedrich Blessing.
    2. Photograph. Courtesy of Feico Glastra van Loon.
c. 860 and 880 Lake Shore Drive, Chicago.
    Under construction. c. 1951.
    Photograph by Hedrich Blessing.

114

117

118

120

To Hilbs: Class of '49

H. Pfeiffer
Martin Tegen
Rudy Tepeda
Martin Reinhaimer
J. Cowhart
Warren Nowaski
Kingley Hanson
Martin W. Glozner
Leonard Brooks Freeman
Henry Kamize Jr.
Kenneth E. Anderson
Jan Albus
P. N. Daswick
Chester Kitt
J. H. Nelson
H. Chalmers
J. Steed
C. Stanfield
E. Tirtle

Seymour Rutkin
John Holcomb
William S. Wagley
David Tamminga
W. J. van der Meer, Jr.
James Ferris
Robert M. Braun
Richard J. Pauliech
Fred E. Wilson Jr.
Kenneth H. Goslin
Walfred Johnson
George S. Fowler

122

4 IIT AS A MODEL OF A UNIVERSITY CAMPUS

The alternative plans for the IIT campus which Mies studied beginning in 1938, show how he worked comparatively in seeking to discover the best solution to a problem. One proposes a campus in which the expression of function is the dominant issue, while the other presents a campus based on regular structure. In choosing the design ordered by structure Mies believed he had achieved a plan which would be clearer for users, better able to guide and accommodate later additions and more expressive of the values of a modern university in relation to the city.

In the sketches for S.R. Crown Hall exhibited here Mies shows the inventiveness that characterized his entire career. Although the final form, structure and expression of the building had been suggested and explored in projects which he had studied for some time, his studies of stairs for the building show Mies considering various possibilities. Not only do these sketches show him dealing with the horizontal plane in terms similar to a wall, they also show a flexibility of approach which at the outset rejects ordinary habits and assumptions.

125.
Ludwig Mies van der Rohe
S. R. Crown Hall, Illinois Institute of
Technology, Chicago.
Under construction. c. 1955.
Photograph by Hedrich Blessing.

126.
Ludwig Mies van der Rohe
Joseph Fujikawa
a. Eight sketch studies for S. R.
   Crown Hall, Illinois Institute of
   Technology.
   Early 1950's.
   Pencil on note paper.
   6″ × 8¼″ (15.1 × 21.1 cm).*
b. Six sketch studies for
   S. R. Crown Hall. Interiors.
   Early 1950's.
   Pencil on note paper.
   5″ × 7¼″ (12.5 × 18.5 cm) and
   6″ × 8¼″ (15.1 × 21.1 cm).*

c. Eight sketch studies for S. R.
   Crown Hall. Early 1950's.
   Pencil on note paper.
   6″ × 8¼″ (15.1 × 21.1 cm).*
d. Eight sketch studies for S. R.
   Crown Hall. Early 1950's.
   Pencil on note paper.
   6″ × 8¼″ (15.1 × 21.1 cm).*

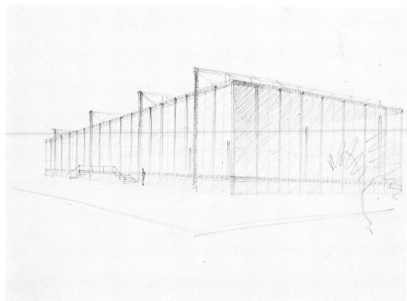

126a

117

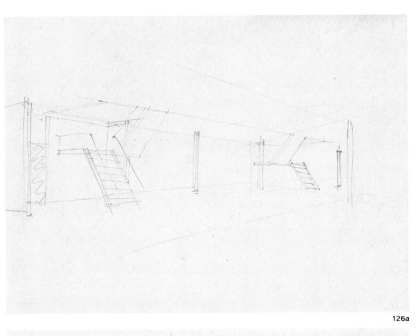

126a

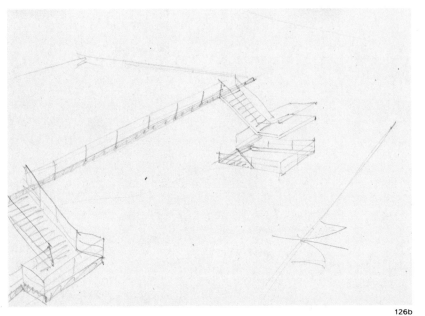

126b

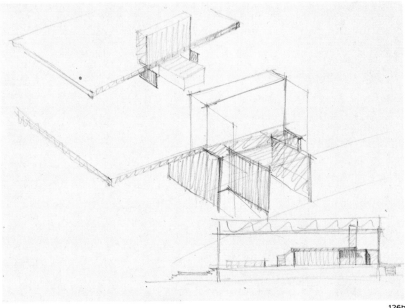

126b

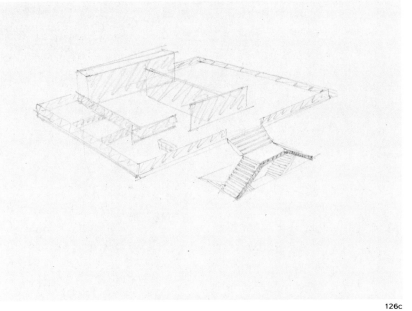

126c

127.
Ludwig Mies van der Rohe
Pace Associates
S. R. Crown Hall. Construction
Drawings. 1955.
a. Sheet A3 — ground floor plan.
b. Sheet A4 — elevations.
c. Sheet A5 — building sections,
   roof and penthouse.
d. Sheet A6 — exterior wall detail.
Pencil on linen.
Lent by the Chicago Historical
Society.

128.
S. R. Crown Hall Dedication, Illinois
Institute of Technology.
30 April 1956.
a. Speaker Walter A. Bletcher, City
   Planning Consultant.
b. John Rettaliata, President of IIT
   with Mies.
c. Mies Giving Rettaliata the Gold
   Key to S. R. Crown Hall.
d. Luncheon Preceding Dedication.
   Mayor Richard J. Daley with John
   Rettaliata and Members of the
   Crown Family.
Photographs by Arthur Siegel.

129.
Three Images of the Illinois Institute
of Technology and Environs.
Early 1940's.
Photograph by Thomas Burleigh.

130.
Ludwig Mies van der Rohe
Buildings on Illinois Institute of
Technology Campus.
a.   Metals and Minerals Building.
     1943.
b.   Alumni Memorial Hall. 1946.
c.   Wishnick Hall Under
     Construction. 1945-46.
d-e. Perlstein Hall Under
     Construction. 1945-46.
f.   S. R. Crown Hall Under
     Construction. 1955-56.
g.   S. R. Crown Hall. Interior. 1956.
Photographs by Hedrich Blessing.

131.
Secretaries
Architecture Department, Illinois
Institute of Technology. Diaries of
the Architecture Department,
Including Visitors, Prospective
Students, Lectures, Publications and
Exhibitions.
a. 6 April 1948–21 July 1950.
b. 1 August 1950–2 December 1954.
3 ring binder with typed entries and
business cards.
9″ × 7″ (22.9 × 17.8 cm).

128b

119

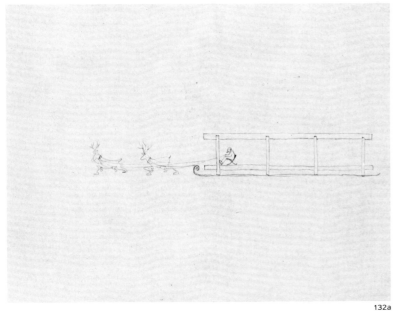

132a

132b

132.
Adrian Gayle
Two Drawings of Mies.
a. Mies on Sleighride.
b. Mies Walking in the Snow.
Photostats of cartoon drawings.
6⅛″ × 8″ (15.3 × 20.3 cm)
and 6″ × 6⅝″ (15.1 × 16.7 cm).
Lent by George Danforth.

133.
Mies with Sculpture of Himself by
Hugo Weber. c. 1961.
8¾″ × 13¼″ (22 × 33.5 cm).
Photograph by Richard Nickel
Lent by Richard Nickel Committee.

134.
Four Images of Werner Graeff with
Mies and George Danforth in
Chicago. October 1968.
Photographer unknown.
Lent by George Danforth.

135.
Experimental photograph of Mies
van der Rohe. c. 1954.
Signed by Mies.
Photographer unknown.
14⅞″ × 11¾″ (36.4 × 29.8 cm).
Lent by Edward A. Duckett.

136.
Inland Architect
American Institute of Architects,
Chicago Chapter. November 1963.
"Mies van der Rohe Twenty-Five
Years of Work in Chicago."
Lent by John Vinci.

137.
Mies and Hilberseimer in Farmer's
Field, Dorchester and 49th, Chicago.
c. 1940.
Photographer unknown.
5″ × 4″ (12.7 × 10.2 cm).
Lent by George Danforth.

138.
Mies and Alfred Caldwell on IIT
Campus.
c. 1947.
Photograph by Thomas Burleigh.

139.
Mies on a Bench at the Beach. 1949.
Photograph by E. Campbell.
Courtesy of Lawrence J. Harrison.

140.
Three Images of a Class Picnic at the
Indiana Dunes. 1949.
Photographs by Mark Finfer.

141.
Three Images of Mies at WTTW-TV,
Chicago, for the Heritage Series.
Early 1960's.
Photographer unknown.
Lent by George Danforth.

142.
Walter Peterhans at a Louis
Armstrong Concert at the Blue Note
Nightclub, Chicago. c. 1950.
Photographer unknown.
7" × 5" (17.6 × 12.5 cm).
Lent by George Danforth.

143.
Norman Ross
"Mies van der Rohe." c. 1957.
Edited version.
Film by Ross-McElroy Productions,
Chicago.

133

134

138

139

5 GRADUATE STUDIES UNDER MIES 1938-1958

In his early graduate teaching, Mies directed students towards abstract issues at the juncture of architectural practice and social values: schools, churches, museums. Problems were studied comparatively and historically to understand the relation between expression and values in other places at other times. Later students became increasingly interested in problems of actual building, and spent less time considering them in terms of their social function. At about the same time these projects became refinements of work Mies had already explored, rather than investigations of ideas that he was then considering. The problems of very large structures received greater attention. They were studied with respect to the most advanced structural techniques available and to the questions of scale. It was assumed that the nature of the problems suggested an appropriate structural order. The architectural solution then became the expression of that order. The major means in solving the question of scale emerged through studies of proportion. These issues have been pursued principally through the influence and teaching of Myron Goldsmith, David Sharpe and the late Fazlur Khan.

192h

122

144.
Anonymous
Graduate.
Regional Planning.
Part of a Replanned City on Hilly
Ground.
Colored inks and wash on
Strathmore board.
40″ × 30″ (101.6 × 76 cm).*

145.
Anonymous
Graduate.
Regional Planning.
a. Chicago, View from Lake
    Michigan to Fox River.
    Proposed Study.
b. Chesapeake Bay/Potomac River
    Area.
    Proposed Study.
Air brush, ink on Strathmore board.
40″ × 30″ (101.6 × 76 cm) each.*

146.
Donald Munson
Warren Spitz
Graduate. Regional Planning.
Regional Study of Chicago. c. 1931.
Four panels a/b/c/d. Existing
Conditions.
Four panels e/f/g/h. Proposed
Solution.
Ink and wash on Strathmore board.
40″ × 30″ (101.6 × 76 cm) each.*

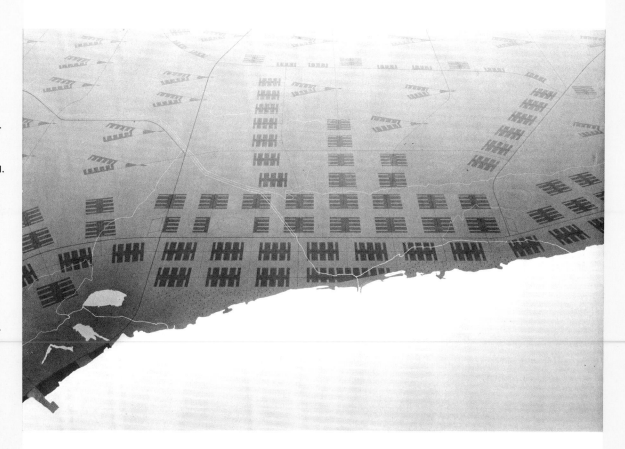

145a

CHICAGO   VIEW FROM LAKE MICHIGAN TO THE FOX RIVER

148a

147.
A. James Speyer
Graduate. Advanced Architecture I
501, 502.
Courthouse Problem. Perspective.
1939.
Collage with pencil on Strathmore
board.
30″ × 40″ (76 x 101.6 cm).*

148.
George Danforth
Graduate. Advanced Architecture I
501, 502. 1941.
a. Wall Problem Composition.
   Collage on Strathmore board.
   20″ × 30″ (51 × 76 cm).
b. Residence with a Court.
   Perspective done under Mies and
   Peterhans.
   Collage with pencil on
   Strathmore board.
   30″ × 40″ (76 × 101.6 cm).

149.
George Danforth (Layout)
Ludwig Mies van der Rohe
(Delineation and Composition)
Graduate. Advanced Architecture I
501, 502.
Residence with a Court. Perspective.
Collage and pencil on illustration
board.
30″ × 40″ (76 × 101.6 cm).

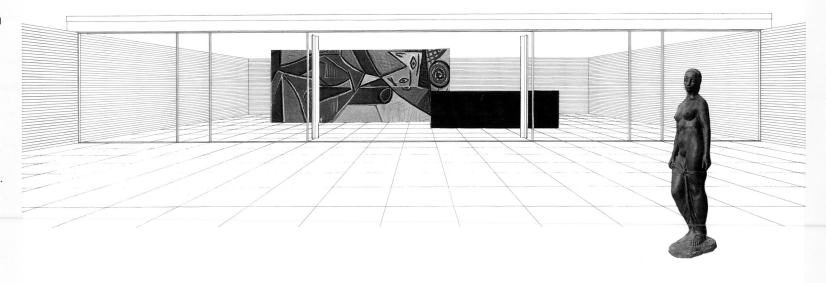

148b

125

150a

150.
Reginald Malcolmson
Graduate. Advanced Architecture I
501, 502.
a. Concert Hall in a Factory. 1947.
    Photo collage on illustration
    board.
    15″ × 31¼″ (38 x 79.5 cm).
b. Skyscraper Studies of Curtain
    Wall. 1948.
    Ink on Strathmore board.
    30″ × 20″ (76 × 51 cm).

151.
Jose Polar
Graduate. Advanced Architecture I
501, 502.
Courthouse Problem. Plans.
1949-50.
Collage on Strathmore board.
20″ × 30″ (51 × 76 cm).*

152.
Gene R. Summers
Graduate. Advanced Architecture
501, 502.
Courthouse Problem. Plans.
8 December 1949.
Collage on Strathmore board.
20″ × 30″ (51 × 76 cm).*

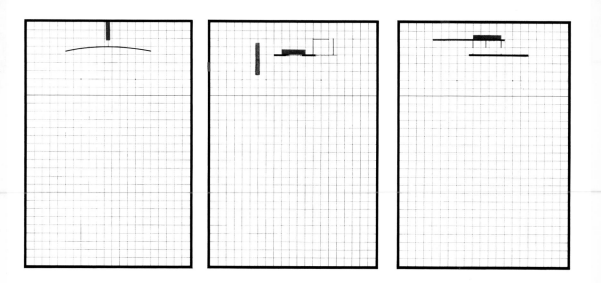

152

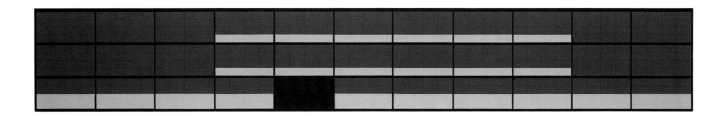

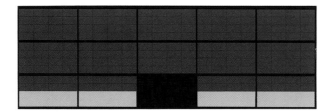

153a

153.
Gene R. Summers
Graduate. Advanced Architecture
501, 502.
Three Story Skeleton Structure.
Elevation Studies.
a. Steel Structure. 13 March 1950.
b. Concrete Structure. 4 April 1950.
Collage on Strathmore board.
30" × 40" (76 × 101.6 cm) each.*

154.
Anonymous
Graduate. Advanced Architecture I.
Courthouse Problem. c. 1950's.
a. Series of three plans.
b. Series of three plans.
Collage on Strathmore board.
20" × 30" (51 × 76 cm) each.*

155.
A. James Speyer
Graduate Thesis. "The Space
Concept in Modern Domestic
Architecture." Various illustrations
from thesis. 1938. Photographs.

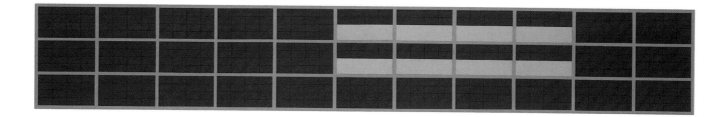

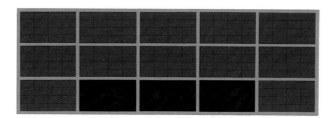

153b

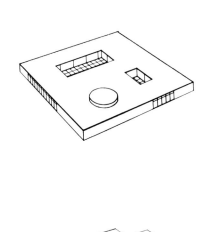

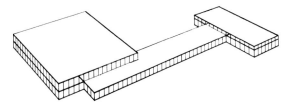

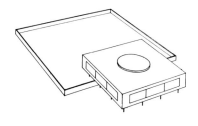

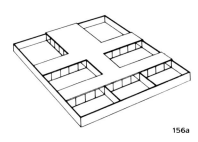

156.
Charles Worley
Graduate Thesis. "A School for Art and Architecture." 1941.
a. Building Types Investigated and Rejected.
b. Front Elevation of the School.
Photographs.

157.
Ludwig Mies van der Rohe
George Danforth
Thirteen Sketches: Museum for a Small City. c. 1939-42.
a-d: 6″ × 8¼″ (15.2 × 21 cm).
e-j: 6″ × 7″ (15.2. × 17.8 cm).
k-m: 8½″ × 13″ (21.5 × 33 cm).

158.
Charles Genther
Graduate Thesis (unfinished).
"Towards a New Architecture."
1942-43.
Various illustrations from thesis.
Photographs.

156a

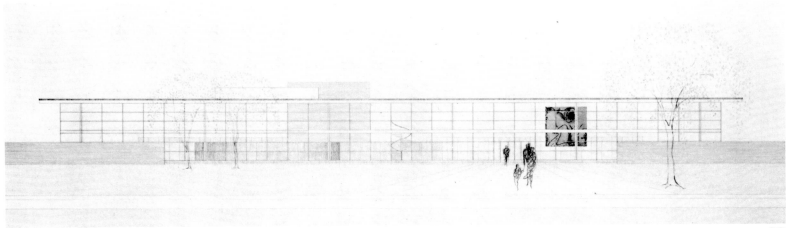

156b

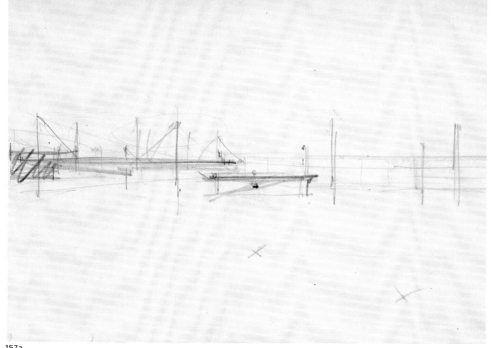

157a

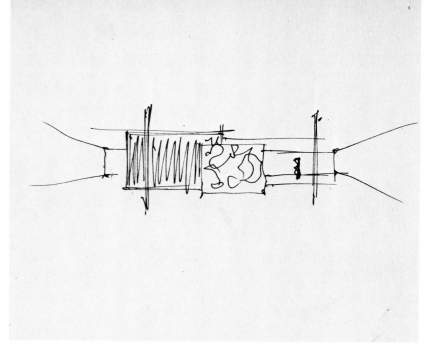

157c

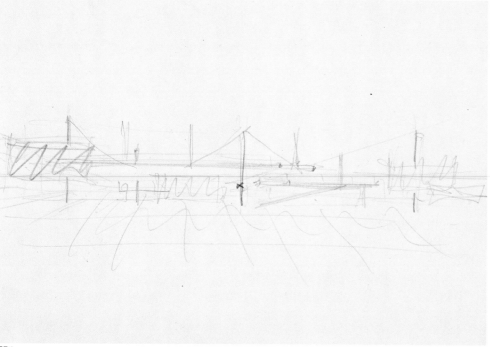

157d

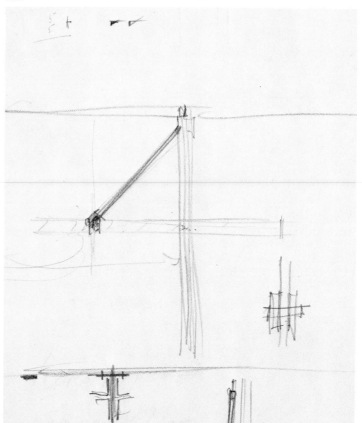

131

157e

159

161a

159.
Daniel Brenner
Graduate Thesis.
"An Art Museum." 1949.
Model-Exterior View.
Photograph.

160.
James Ferris
Graduate Thesis.
"The Replanning of a University
Campus." 1951.
Model-View of the Campus Looking
West Along University Avenue.
Photograph.

161.
Wei Tung Lo
Graduate Thesis.
"University Administration Building."
1951.
a. Model-Perspective.
b. Administration Building with
   Surrounding Buildings.
Photographs.

162.
Jose Polar
Graduate Thesis.
"The Student Dining Hall." 1951.
Model-Perspective.
Photograph.

163.
Gene R. Summers
Graduate Thesis.
"A Fieldhouse." 1951.
a. Plan.
b. Elevation.
Photographs.

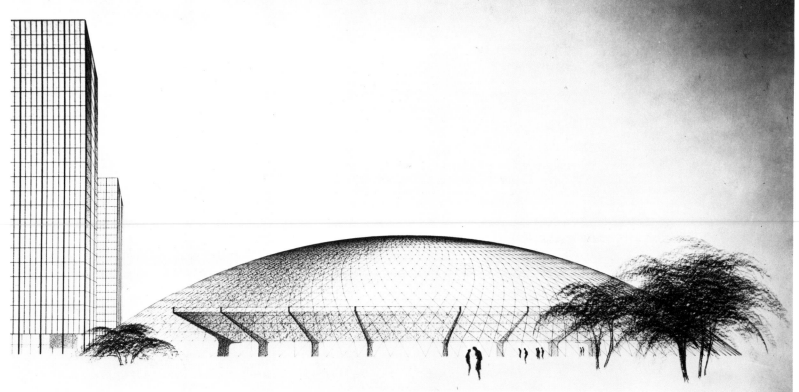

163b

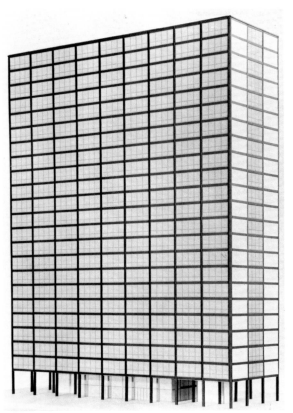

164c

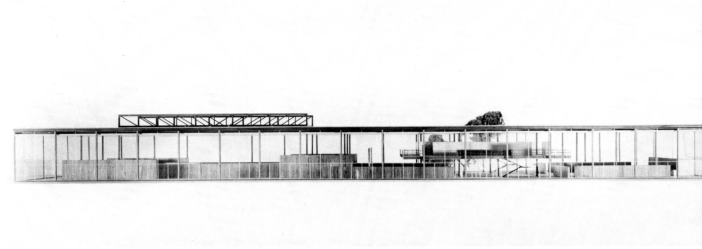

165a

164.
David J. Tamminga
Graduate Thesis.
"Student Housing for a University
Campus." 1951.
a. Tall Concrete Structure.
b. Tall Steel Structure — Study I.
c. Dormitory — General View.
d. Dormitory Grouping.
Photographs.

165.
Yau Chun Wong
Graduate Thesis.
"The Student Union." 1951.
a. Model — Side (south or north)
   View.
b. Model — General View.
Photograph.

166.
John Sugden
Graduate Thesis.
"An Industrial Exhibition Hall." 1952.
Model — Front Elevation.
Photograph.

167.
Edmond N. Zisook
Graduate Thesis.
"A Recreation and Social Center for
Neighborhood Community." 1952.
Model — Front Elevation.
Photograph.

168.
Joseph Fujikawa
Graduate Thesis.
"A Suburban Shopping Center."
1953.
a. Store — Ground Floor Plan.
b. Perspective.
Pencil on Strathmore board.
30" × 40" (76 x 101.6 cm) each.

168b

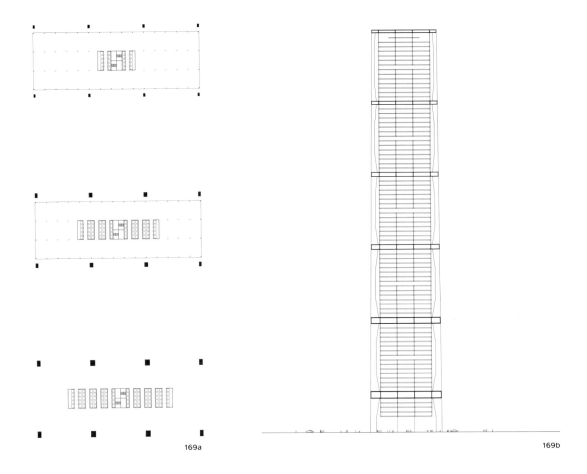

169a

169b

169.
Myron Goldsmith
Graduate Thesis.
"The Tall Building: The Effects of Scale." 1953.
a. Plans.
b. Elevation.
c. Perspective.
d. Alternate Elevations.
Ink on Strathmore board.
30" × 40" (76 x 101.6 cm) each.

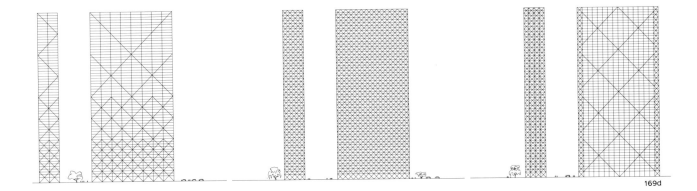

169d

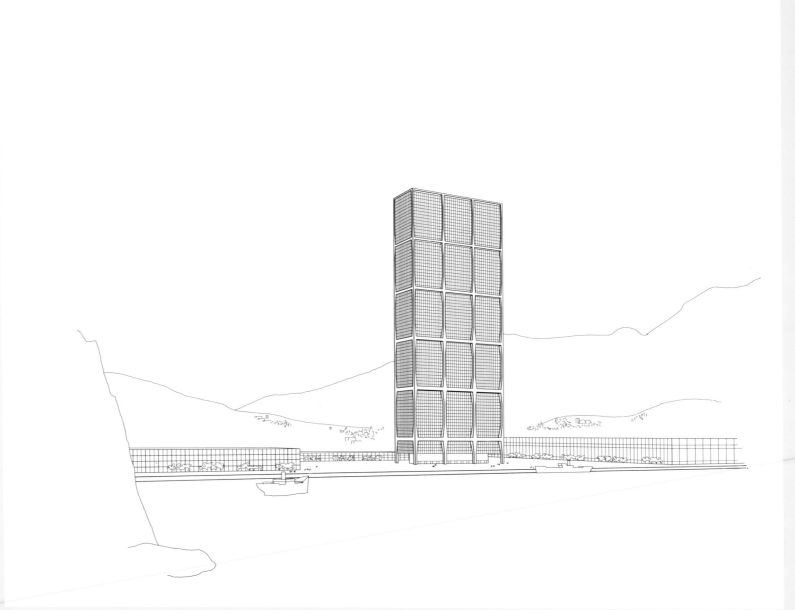

169c

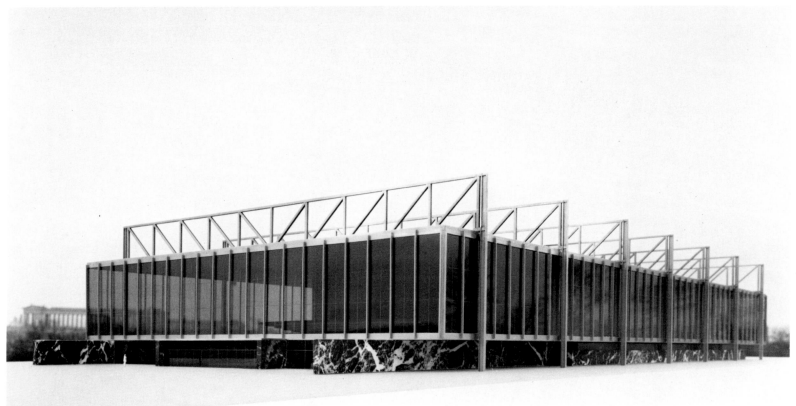

170a

170.
David Haid
Graduate Thesis.
"An Art Center." 1953.
a. Model Exterior.
b. Model Interior.
Photographs by Hedrich Blessing.

171.
Jacques Brownson
Graduate Thesis.
"A Steel and Glass House." 1954.
a. Floor Plan.
b. Roof Hanger Section.
Ink on Strathmore board. Redrawn
by Elizabeth Kunin. 1986.
30" × 20" (76 x 51 cm) each.
c. East Elevation.
Photograph.

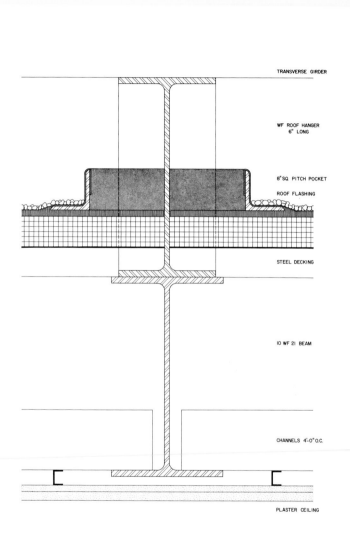

TRANSVERSE GIRDER

WF ROOF HANGER
6" LONG

8" SQ. PITCH POCKET

ROOF FLASHING

STEEL DECKING

IO WF 21 BEAM

CHANNELS 4'-0" O.C.

PLASTER CEILING

ROOF HANGER SECTION

171a

171b

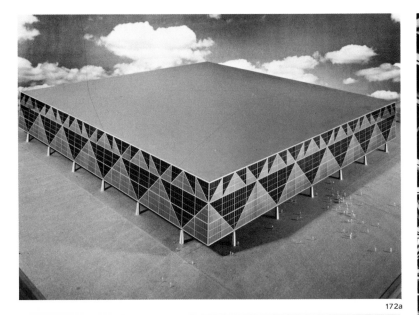

172a

172b

172c

172.
Pao Chi Chang
Henry Kanazawa
Yujiro Miwa
Graduate Thesis.
"A Convention Hall." 1954.
a. Model — Bird's Eye View.
b. Model — Exterior Corner Detail.
c. Model — Interior Corner Detail.
d. Structural System. Perspective
    Section.
e. Preliminary Studies of Black,
    Brown and Tan Granite.
f. Elevation Studies in Two and
    Three Colors.
Photographs a-c., by Hedrich
Blessing.

173.
Antonio Casimir Ramos
Jacob Karl Viks
Graduate Thesis.
"Interior Studies of a Large Hall."
1955.
A Concert Hall — Interior View.
Photograph.

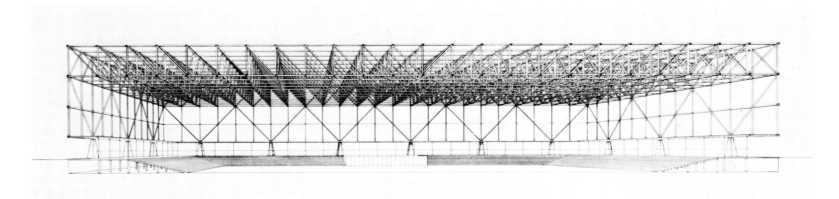

172d

173

174.
Jan Lippert
Graduate Thesis.
"A Museum." 1956.
Model — Exterior View.
Photograph.

175

175.
Reginald Malcolmson
Graduate Thesis.
"A Theatre." 1957.
Elevation.
Collage on Strathmore board.
30" × 40" (76 × 101.6 cm).

176.
Peter Carter
Graduate Thesis.
"An Art Museum." 1958.
a. Structural Framing. Perspective.
b. Model — Exterior View.
Photographs.

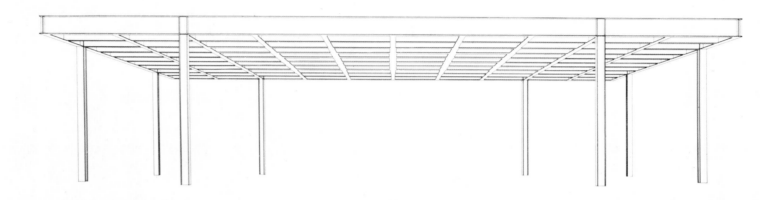

176a

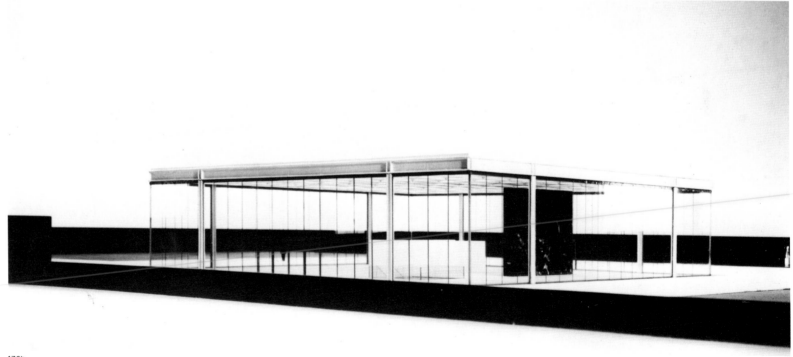

176b

143

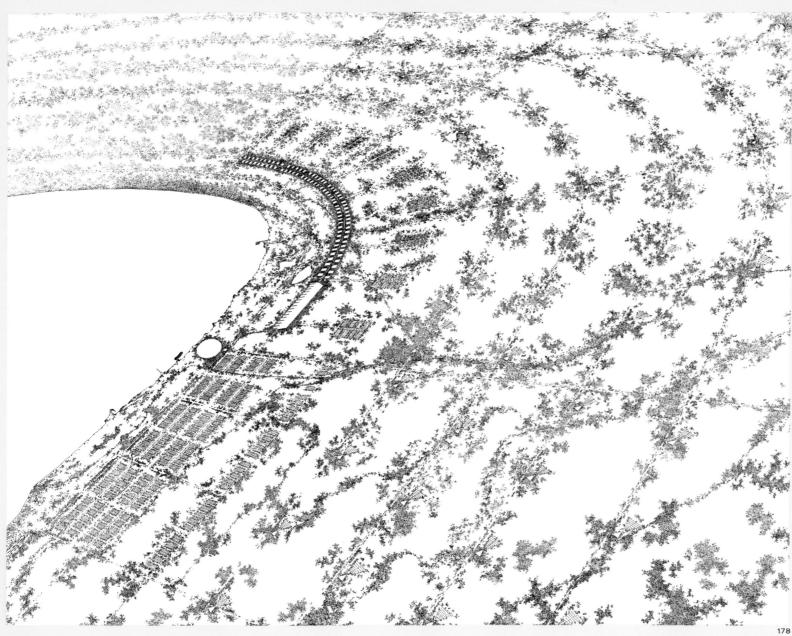

177.
Alfred Caldwell
Regional Park Plan. 1957.
Pencil on Strathmore board.
19⅛″ × 24″ (48.7 × 60.9 cm).
Collection: American Friends of the
CCA on loan to Centre Canadien
d'Architecture/Canadian Centre for
Architecture, Montréal

178.
Alfred Caldwell
A Proposed Plan for Chicago. 1942.
Pencil on Strathmore board.
29⅞″ × 39⅞″ (76 × 101.5 cm).
Collection: American Friends of the
CCA on loan to Centre Canadien
d'Architecture/Canadian Centre for
Architecture, Montréal

179.
Alfred Caldwell
Landscape Perspective of Small
Houses and School. 1959.
Pencil on Strathmore board.
17¾″ × 23⅞″ (45 × 60.8 cm).
Collection: American Friends of the
CCA on loan to Centre Canadien
d'Architecture/Canadian Centre for
Architecture, Montréal

178

180.
Phil Hart and others
Advanced Architecture I.
a-b. 50' × 50' House Problem. c.
        1951.
Model in Landscape Setting.
Photographs by Hedrich Blessing.

181.
Abdel-Monheim Hassan Kamel
Graduate Thesis.
"Concert Hall." 1949.
Model in Open House Exhibit.
Photograph.
Courtesy of George Danforth.

182.
Convention Hall Project, Chicago.
1953.
Color photograph of collage in the
collection of Museum of Modern Art.

180a

180b

188

189

183.
Open House Exhibit, Alumni Memorial Hall, Illinois Institute of Technology. c. 1947.
Photograph by Feico Glastra van Loon.

184.
Open House, Senior Rooms, Alumni Memorial Hall, Illinois Institute of Technology. 300' × 300' Long Span Structure (Brenner, Dunlap and Malcolmson). 1947–48.
Photograph by Reginald Malcolmson.

185.
Open House Exhibit, Alumni Memorial Hall, Illinois Institute of Technology. Kamel's Model. 1947–48.
Photograph by Reginald Malcolmson.

186.
Hilberseimer's Graduate Seminar. 1948.
Photographer unknown.
Courtesy of Reginald Malcolmson.

187.
Two Images of Mies Studying Model With Students. c. 1948–49.
Photographer unknown.
Courtesy of Feico Glastra van Loon.

188.
Three images of Hilberseimer's Day Party. 21 December 1961.
Color photographs.
2⅜" × 3⅜" (6.6 × 8.7 cm).
Lent by George Danforth.

189.
Eight Images of Mies's 75th Birthday Party at Charles Genther's Apartment, 860 Lake Shore Drive, Chicago. 1961.
Polaroid photographs.
Lent by George Danforth.

190.
Ludwig Mies van der Rohe
Philip Johnson
The Seagram Building, New York. 1957.
Photograph by Malcolm Smith.
Lent by John Burgee Architects with Philip Johnson.

191.
Ludwig Mies van der Rohe
Ludwig Hilberseimer
Alfred Caldwell
Lafayette Park. c. 1958.
Model — Bird's Eye View.
Photograph by Hedrich Blessing.

146

192.
Ludwig Mies Van der Rohe
a. Promontory Apartments,
   Chicago. 1949.
   Photograph by Hedrich Blessing.
b. Farnsworth House, Plano, Illinois.
   1950.
   Photograph by Hedrich Blessing.
c. 860 and 880 Lake Shore Drive,
   Chicago. 1951.
   Photograph by Hedrich Blessing.
d. National Theatre of the City of
   Mannheim, Project. 1953.
   Photograph by Hedrich Blessing.
e. S.R. Crown Hall, Illinois Institute
   of Technology. 1956.
   Photograph by Hedrich Blessing.
f. Bacardi Office Building Project,
   Santiago de Cuba. 1957.
   Model.
   Photograph by Hedrich Blessing.
g. The Federal Center, Chicago.
   1964.
   Photograph by Hedrich Blessing.

192a

192b

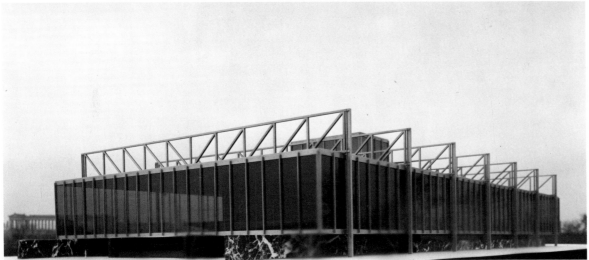

192d

192f

IIT COURSES IN ARCHITECTURE, 1938–1958

Note: Odd numbered courses usually indicate the Fall Semester and even numbered courses usually indicate the Spring Semester.

	'38-'39	'39-'40	'40-'41	'41-'42	'42-'43	'43-'44	'44-'45	'45-'46	'46-'47	'47-'48	'48-'49	'49-'50	'50-'51	'51-'52	'52-'53	'53-'54	'54-'55	'55-'56	'56-'57	'57-'58	
101		Applied Descriptive Geometry					Axonometric Geometry				Axonometric Projection										101
102		Applied Descriptive Geometry																			102
103													Axonometric Projection								103
104													Applied Descriptive Geometry								104
105	Freehand Drawing										Life Drawing										105
106	Freehand Drawing										Life Drawing										106
107	Arch.	Elementary Drafting																			107
108	Arch.	Elementary Drafting					Perspective Drawing														108
109		Arch. Theory and Visual Training											Life Drawing								109
110													Life Drawing								110
201	Arch. Const.																				201
202	Arch. Const.																				202
203		Architectural History																			203
204		Architectural History																			204
205	Freehand Drawing										Life Drawing										205
206	Freehand Drawing										Life Drawing										206
207		Materials and Construction																			207
208		Materials and Construction																			208
209		Architectural Theory and Visual Training											Architectural History								209
210		Arch. Theory and Visual Training											Architectural History								210
211		Arch. Theory and Visual Training		Visual Training																	211
212				Visual Training																	212
213													Materials and Construction								213
214													Materials and Construction								214
215													Life Drawing								215
216													Life Drawing								216

FRESHMAN

SOPHOMORE

	'38-'39	'39-'40	'40-'41	'41-'42	'42-'43	'43-'44	'44-'45	'45-'46	'46-'47	'47-'48	'48-'49	'49-'50	'50-'51	'51-'52	'52-'53	'53-'54	'54-'55	'55-'56	'56-'57	'57-'58	

JUNIOR

- 301 — Arch. Practice ('49-'50)
- 302 — Arch. Practice ('49-'50)
- 303 — Architectural History ('39-'40–'42-'43); Architectural Practice ('50-'51 onward)
- 304 — Architectural History ('39-'40–'42-'43); Architectural Practice ('50-'51 onward)
- 305 — Freehand Drawing ('39-'40); Visual Training ('49-'50–; '54-'55 onward)
- 306 — Visual Training ('49-'50–; '54-'55 onward)
- 307 — Theory and Design of Dwellings and Housing ('39-'40); Dwellings ('43-'44); Housing ('50-'51)
- 308 — Theory and Design of Dwellings and Housing ('39-'40); Community and Public Buildings ('41-'42)
- 309 — Housing and Community Buildings ('53-'54 onward)
- 310 — Housing Development ('53-'54 onward)
- 311 — Visual Training ('38-'39); Architectural Construction ('40-'41)
- 312 — Visual Training ('38-'39); Reinf. Conc. Const. ('39-'40); Architectural Construction ('40-'41)
- 313 — Arch. Const. ('38-'39); Analysis of Art ('42-'43)
- 314 — Arch. Const. ('38-'39); Analysis of Art ('42-'43)

SENIOR

- 401 — Architectural Practice ('38-'39)
- 402 — Architectural Practice ('38-'39)
- 403 — Architectural History ('39-'40–'42-'43); Architecture ('50-'51 onward)
- 404 — Architectural History ('39-'40–'42-'43); Architecture ('50-'51 onward)
- 405 — Seminar ('53-'54)
- 406 — Seminar ('53-'54)
- 407 — Architecture ('38-'39)
- 408 — Architecture ('38-'39)
- 409 — City Planning ('38-'39); Theory of City Planning ('51-'52)
- 410 — City Planning ('38-'39); Theory of City Planning ('51-'52)
- 411 — Arch. Theory and Arch. and Culture ('39-'40); Analysis of Art ('41-'42)
- 412 — Arch. Theory and Arch. and Culture ('39-'40); Analysis of Art ('41-'42)
- 413 — History and Analysis of Art ('50-'51); Analysis of Art ('53-'54)
- 414 — History and Analysis of Art ('50-'51); Analysis of Art ('53-'54)

Course	Course Title	Years
415	Hist. and Analysis of Art	'51-'52 to '52-'53
415	Analysis of Art	'53-'54 to '57-'58
416	Hist. and Analysis of Art	'51-'52 to '52-'53
416	Analysis of Art	'53-'54 to '57-'58
417	Technics and Architecture	'53-'54 to '57-'58
418	Technics and Architecture	'53-'54 to '57-'58
420	Applied City Planning	'53-'54 to '57-'58
443	Architecture	'53-'54 to '57-'58
444	Architecture	'53-'54 to '57-'58
453	Architecture	'51-'52 to '52-'53
454	Architecture	'51-'52 to '52-'53
455	Architecture	'50-'51 to '52-'53
456	Architecture	'50-'51 to '52-'53
458	Theory of Regional Planning	'50-'51 to '52-'53
459	Theory of Regional Planning	'53-'54 to '57-'58
460	Applied Regional Planning	'53-'54 to '57-'58
461	Physical Factors of Planning: Analysis and Representation	'53-'54 to '57-'58
462	Physical Factors of Planning: Analysis and Representation	'53-'54 to '57-'58
463	History and Analysis of Cities	'53-'54 to '57-'58
464	Architecture of Cities	'53-'54 to '57-'58
465	City Planning Practice	'53-'54 to '57-'58
466	City Planning Practice	'53-'54 to '57-'58
493	Seminar	'49-'50 to '51-'52
494	Seminar	'48-'49 to '51-'52

SENIOR II ARCHITECTURE

SENIOR III PLANNING

153

| | '38-'39 | '39-'40 | '40-'41 | '41-'42 | '42-'43 | '43-'44 | '44-'45 | '45-'46 | '46-'47 | '47-'48 | '48-'49 | '49-'50 | '50-'51 | '51-'52 | '52-'53 | '53-'54 | '54-'55 | '55-'56 | '56-'57 | '57-'58 | |

501 — Advanced Architecture I ... 501

502 — Advanced Architecture I ... 502

503 — Theory of Dwelling and Housing ... 503

504 — Theory of Dwelling and Housing ... 504

505 — Theory of City Planning ... 505

506 — Theory of City Planning ... 506

507 — Theory of Regional Planning ... 507

508 — Theory of Regional Planning ... 508

509 — Applied City Planning ... 509

510 — Applied City Planning ... 510

511 — Applied Regional Planning ... 511

512 — Applied Regional Planning ... 512

521 — Advanced Architecture ... 521

522 — Advanced Architecture ... 522

591 — Thesis ... 591

592 — Thesis ... 592

593 — Special Problems ... 593

594 — Special Problems ... 594

595 — Special Problems ... 595

597 — Special Problems ... 597

599 — Thesis ... 599

600 — Ph.D. ... 600

691 — Ph.D. ... 691

692 — Ph.D. ... 692

699 — Ph.D. ... 699

GRADUATE

IIT ARCHITECTURE FACULTY AND STUDENTS, 1938–1958

Compiled by Donna J. Junkroski

FACULTY

COURSES TAUGHT WITH DATES IN PARENTHESES.

ANSCHUETZ, KLAUS (55-57) 461, 462
BAR, NELLIE (50-51) 215, 216; (50-58) 109,110
BLUESTEIN, EARL (46-52) 308; (48-52) 307; (46-49) 410; (52-55) 409, 410; (53-55) 420, 461, 462
BRENNER, DANIEL (48-50) 407, 408; (48-51) 493, 494; (50-63) 403, 404; (53-59) 417, 418; (55-56) 413, 416
BROWNSON, JACQUES (48-52) 409, 410; (52-55) 103, 104, 107, 108; (55-58) 309, 310
CALDWELL, ALFRED (45-50) 203, 204, 207; (45-60) 311, 312; (46-47) 208; (47-48) 208; (50-58) 209, 210, 213, 214
DANFORTH, GEORGE E. (40-43) 101,102, 107, 108; (46-47) 102, 108; (46-49) 207, 208; (49-52) 211, 212; (50-52) 305, 306; (52-53) 403, 404
DEARSTYNE, HOWARD (57-58) 413, 414, 415, 416, 443, 444
DORNBUSCH, CHARLES (38-39) 201, 202, 203, 313, 314; (39-40) 307, 308, 312, 402, 410
DUCKETT, EDWARD (45-49) 101, 107; (46-49) 102, 108
DUNLAP, WILLIAM E. (49-50) 207; (50-51) 103, 104, 107, 108
ERNST, HENRY (55-58) 303, 304
FORSBERG, ELMER (45-50) 105, 205; (46-50) 106, 206
HARPER, STERLING (38-39) 102, 402; (38-40) 401; (38-39) 101, 107, 204
HILBERSEIMER, LUDWIG (38-42) 409; (38-50) 307, 308, 410; (39-40) 303, 304; (40-43) 507; (41-42) 504, 506, 512, 591; (41-43) 503, 505; (43-44) 313, 411; (43-45) 312, 314; (43-50) 409; (44-45) 107,108, 311, 412, 509, 510; (44-46) 503, 508; (45-46) 102, 505, 506, 591; (45-47) 501; (46-47) 510; (46-48) 592; (46-49) 504; (47-48) 506, 512; (47-49) 507, 594; (47-55) 508; (47-58) 509; (47-59) 505; (49-50) 510; (49-51) 511, 595; (49-54) 699; (50-51) 593; (50-53) 455, 456, 458, 594; (51-52) 512, 599; (52-53) 510, 511; (53- 60) 560; (53-61) 459; (54-55) 599;

(55-57) 510; (55-58) 512; (55-59) 511; (56-57) 591; (56-58) 508, 599; (57-58) 506, 692
HOFGESANG, JAMES (49-50) 101, 102; (49-52) 107, 108; (50-52) 103, 104
HOSKINS, TOM (42-45) 402; (43-44) 401
KREHBIEL, ALBERT A. (38-40) 305; (38-45) 105, 106, 205, 206
KROFTA, JOSEPH (55-56) 104, 108; (56-58) 409, 420
LILIBRIDGE, ROBERT (55-58) 465; (55-58) 466; (57-58) 408
MALCOLMSON, REGINALD (49-50) 307, 308, 311, 312; (52-53) 307, 308; (53-55) 309, 310; (53-60) 464; (53-61) 463; (54-55) 405; (55-56) 420, 462, 501, 521, 522, 591; (55-58) 409; (57- 58) 420
MELL, ALFRED (38-39) 207; (39-40) 101, 102, 107, 108; (40-41) 308; (40-42) 307; (40-43) 312; (40-44) 311; (41-43) 204, 208; (42-44) 203, 207
MIES VAN DER ROHE, LUDWIG (38-39) 107; (38-47) 407, 408; (39-55) 501; (39-55) 502; (42-43) 401, 409, 411, 506, 508, 509, 511, 592; (42-46) 591; (43-44) 412, 503, 504; (43-45) 211; (43- 46) 505; (44-45) 101, 102, 203, 204, 207, 208, 212, 401; (45-46) 503, 508; (46-47) 592; (47-55) 591; (48-54) 521, 599; (49-53) 522; (53-54) 597; (55-56) 597, 599; 599; (56- 58) 501, 502, 521; (56-57) 522; (57-58) 503, 510, 591, 592, 599, 600
OSBORN, ADDIS (45-46) 106, 206
PETERHANS, WALTER (38-39) 108, 311, 312; (39-41) 109; (39-42) 210, 403, 404, 411; (39-43) 211, 412; (40-42) 303, 304; (41- 43) 212; (42-43) 313, 314; (42-45) 102; (44-45) 101; (44-50) 411, 412; (45-59) 211; (46-50) 314; (46-59) 212; (48-52) 593; (49-51) 594; (49-59) 305, 306; (50-55) 413, 414; (51- 55) 415, 416; (55-56) 593, 594; (56-57) 414, 415, 416; (56- 58) 597
PRIESTLEY, WILLIAM (41-42) 203, 207; (54-56) 521; (55-56) 502, 522, 591
ROCKWELL, MATTHEW (53-55) 465, 466
RODGERS, JOHN B. (38-39) 202; (38-41) 208; (38-42) 207; (39-41) 203, 204; (40-42) 401, 402; (41-42) 407, 408
SHUMA, WILLIAM F. (46-49) 401, 402
SPEYER, A. JAMES (46-47) 501; (46-50) 407, 408; (47-51)

495; (48- 51) 493; (50-51) 403, 404; (51-53) 453, 454; (53-57) 443, 444
STOPA, WALTER (49-50) 301, 302, 402; (50-55) 303, 304
TAMMINGA, DAVID J. (50-52) 213, 214
TURCK (HILL), DOROTHY (54-58) 103, 107; (56-58) 104, 108
WALKER, ROBIN (57-58) 462
WIEGHARDT, PAUL (50-58) 215, 216

STUDENTS

COURSES TAKEN WITH DATES IN PARENTHESES.

AARON, L. (51-52) 103, 104, 107, 108; (52-53) 209, 210, 211, 212, 213, 214, 215; (53-54) 309, 310, 311, 312; (54-55) 403, 404, 409, 413, 414, 420; (55-56) 415, 416, 417, 418, 443, 444
ABE, T. (44-45) 106, 204, 206, 208, 212; (45-46) 205, 307, 311, 313; (46-47) 407, 409, 411
ABELL, J. (49-50) 101, 102, 105, 106, 107, 108; (50-51) 209, 210, 211, 212, 213, 214, 215 216; (51-52) 303, 305, 306, 307, 308, 311, 312; (52-53) 403, 404, 409, 410, 413, 414; (53-54) 459, 460, 461, 462, 463, 464, 465, 466
ADAMS, W. (46-47) 102, 106, 108, 203, 205, 211; (48-49) 307, 308, 311, 312, 313, 314; (49-50) 301, 302, 407, 408, 409, 410, 411, 412, 493, 494; (50-51) 211
AHERN, T. (42-43) 101, 102, 107, 108, 204
AIKENS, W. (49-50) 101, 102, 105, 106, 107, 108; (50-51) 209, 210, 211, 212, 213, 214, 215, 216; (51-52) 303, 304, 305, 306, 307, 308, 311, 312; (52-53) 403, 404, 409, 410, 413, 414; (53-54) 459, 460, 461, 462, 463, 464, 465, 466
AKERMAN, R. (57-58) 502, 597
ALBANO, J. (44-45) 212; (45-46) 311
ALBERS, G. (48-49) 407, 408, 409, 501, 502, 505, 506, 510; (49- 50) 508, 511, 521, 591, 593, 595
ALBERT, A. (50-51) 103, 107, 109, 215
ALLEN, D. (39-40) 108
ALONGI, F. (48-49) 101, 102, 105, 106, 107, 108; (49-50)

203, 204, 205, 206, 207, 208, 211, 212
ALPER, Z. (45-46) 101, 102, 107, 203, 205, 207, 211; (46-47) 307, 308, 311, 312, 313, 314; (47-48) 402, 408, 410, 412, 494
ALROTH, F. (52-53) 110
ALSCHULER, J. (38-39) 201, 203, 205, 207, 202, 204, 206, 208, 312
AMES, H. (47-48) 204, 206, 208, 212; (48-49) 307, 308, 311, 312, 313, 314; (49-50) 301, 302, 407, 408, 409, 410, 411, 412, 493, 494
AMES, R. (47-48) 102, 108, 206; (48-49) 203, 204, 205, 207, 208, 211, 212; (49-50) 301, 302, 305, 306, 307, 308, 311, 312, 313, 314; (50-51) 403, 404, 409, 410, 413, 414; (51-52) 453, 454
ANANTASANT, V. (54-55) 462, 464, 505, 508, 509; (55-56) 461, 463, 464, 466, 510, 511, 512, 591; (56-57) 599
ANASCHUETZ, K. (54-55) 462, 464, 466, 501, 505
ANDAYA, M. (57-58) 103, 104, 107, 108, 109, 110
ANDERSON, B. (44-45) 101, 102, 105, 106, 108; (45-46) 203, 205, 207, 211; (46-47) 307, 311, 313, 314
ANDERSON, C. (38-39) 101, 105, 107, 202, 203, 204, 205, 206, 207, 208, 312; (39-40) 205; (41-42) 303, 304, 307, 308, 311, 312; (46-47) 307, 308, 311, 312, 313, 314; (47-48) 212, 402, 408, 410, 412, 494
ANDERSON, D. (47-48) 204, 206, 208, 212; (48-49) 106, 307, 308, 311, 312, 313, 314; (49-50) 301, 302, 407, 408, 409, 410, 411, 412, 493, 494
ANDERSON, E. (44-45) 102, 106; (45-46) 203, 205, 207, 211; (46- 47) 307, 308, 311, 312, 313, 314; (47-48) 402, 408, 410, 412, 494
ANDERSON, HAROLD (48-49) 101,102, 105, 106, 107, 108; (49-50) 203, 204, 205, 206, 207, 208, 211, 212; (50-51) 303, 304, 305, 306, 307, 308, 311, 312; (51-52) 403, 404, 409, 410, 413, 414
ANDERSON, HARRY (48-49) 101, 102, 105, 106, 107, 108; (49-50) 203, 204, 205, 206, 207, 208, 211, 212; (50-51) 303, 304, 305, 306, 307, 308, 311, 312; (51-52) 403, 404, 409, 410, 413, 414; (52-53) 415, 416, 453, 454, 455, 456, 458
ANDERSON, JOHN I. (56-57) 103, 104, 107, 108, 109;

SOLVED PROBLEMS: A DEMAND ON OUR BUILDING METHODS

A lecture at the public convention of the *Bund Deutscher Architekten* 12 December 1923 in the large lecture hall of the Museum for Applied Arts, Berlin, Prinz Albrechtstr. 8. Published in *Bauwelt* 14. 1923. No. 52, p. 719. Translated by Rolf Achilles.

On the farm it is customary to till weed-infested fields without regard to those few blades of grass which still find the energy to survive.

We too are also left with no other choice if we are truly to strive for a new sense of construction.

You are all aware of course of the condition of our buildings and yet I would like to remind you of the fully petrified nonsense along the Kurfürstendam and Dahlem.

I have tried in vain to discover the reason for these buildings. They are neither liveable, economical, nor functional and yet they are to serve as home for the people of our age.

We have not been held in very high esteem, if one really believes that these boxes can fulfill our living needs.

No attempt has been made to grasp and shape, in a basic manner, our varying needs.

Our inner needs have been overlooked and it was thought that a clever juggling of historical elements would suffice.

The condition of these buildings is mendacious, dumb and injurious. On the contrary, we demand of buildings today:

Uncompromising truthfulness and renunciation of all formal lies.

We further demand:

That all planning of housing be dictated by the way we live.

A rational organization is to be sought and the application of new technical means towards this end is a self-evident presumption.

If we fulfill these demands, then the housing of our age is formed.

Since the rental unit is only a multiplicity of individual houses we find that here also the same type and quantity of organic housing is formed. This determines the manner of the housing block.

I cannot show you any illustrations of newer structures which meet these demands because even the new attempts have not gone beyond mere formalities.

To lift your sights over the historical and aesthetic rubble heap of Europe and direct you towards primary and functional housing, I have assembled pictures of buildings which stand outside the greco-roman culture sphere.

I have done this on purpose, because an ax bite in Hildesheim lies closer to my heart than a chisel hole in Athens.

I now show you housing, the structure of which is clearly dictated by function and material.

1. Teepee

    This is the typical dwelling of a nomad. Light and transportable.

2. Leaf Hut

    This is the leaf hut of an Indian. Have you ever seen anything more complete in fulfilling its function and in its use of material? Is this not the involution of jungle shadows?

3. Eskimo House

    Now I lead you to night and ice. Here, moss and seal fur have become the building materials. Walrus ribs form the roof construction.

4. Igloo

We're going farther north. The house of a Central eskimo. Here there is only snow and ice. And still man builds.

5. Summer tent of an Eskimo

This fellow also has a summer villa. The construction materials are skin and bones. From the quiet and solitude of the north I lead you to turbulent medieval Flanders.

6. Castle of the Dukes of Flanders, Ghent

Here, the house has become a fortress.

7. Farm

In the lower German plains stands the house of the German farmer. It's necessities of life: house, stall and hayloft are met in this one structure.

What I have shown you in illustrations meets all the requirements of its inhabitants. We demand nothing more for ourselves. Only timely materials. Since there are no buildings which so completely meet the needs of man today I can only show you a structure from a related area which has been only recently perceived and meets the requirements which I also long for and strive towards in our own housing.

8. Imperator (Luxury Liner, Hamburg-America Line).

Here, you see floating mass housing created out of the needs and materials of our age.

Here I ask again:

Have you ever seen anything more complete in its fulfillment of function and justification of materials?

We would be envied if we had structures which justified our main land needs in such a way.

Only when we experience the needs and means of our age in such a primeval way will we have a new sense of structure. To awaken a consciousness for these things is the purpose of my short talk.

EXPLANATION OF THE EDUCATIONAL PROGRAM

With the following prospectus Mies defined his educational program for the School of Architecture at Armour Institute of Technology in the winter of 1937–1938.

The goal of an Architectural School is to train men who can create organic architecture.

Such men must be able to design structures constructed of modern technical means to serve the specific requirements of existing society. They must also be able to bring these structures within the sphere of art by ordering and proportioning them in relation to their functions, and forming them to express the means employed, the purposes served, and the spirit of the times.

In order to accomplish this, these men must not only be trained in the essentials of construction, professional knowledge and in the creation of architectural form, but they must also develop a realistic insight into the material and spiritual needs of their contemporaries, so that they may be able to create architecture which fittingly fulfills these needs.

Finally, they must be given the opportunity to acquire a basic architectural philosophy and fundamental creative principles which will guide them in their task of creating living architecture. The accompanying program is intended to provide an education which achieves this purpose.

The period of study is divided into three progressive stages, namely: MEANS, PURPOSES, AND PLANNING AND CREATING, with a short period of preparatory training. Parallel and complementary to this creative education, *general theory* and *professional training* will be studied. The subjects in these latter two divisions will be timed to prepare the students for each successive step in his creative development.

Work in mathematics, the natural sciences, and drawing, in these two divisions will be begun before the principal course of study begins. This is the preparatory training referred to above and is indicated on the program by raising these subjects in the two columns at the extreme left of the program in advance of all other subjects. This preparatory training is to teach the students to draw, to see proportions and to understand the rudiments of physics before starting the study of structural means.

The subjects in the column design[at]ed *General Theory* are designed to give the student the necessary scientific and cultural background which will give him the knowledge, the sense of proportion and the historical perspective necessary in his progress through the other stages of his education. Only those aspects of these subjects which have a direct bearing on architecture will be treated.

The subjects in the column designated *Professional Training* cover the specialized architectural knowledge which the student will require to give him the technical proficiency necessary to carry on his creative work in the school and take his place in his profession upon graduation. The first major stage of the student's education entitled *Means*, covers a thorough and systematic study of the principal building materials, their qualities and their proper use in building. The student's work in his parallel course in Natural Science will be arranged to help him make this investigation. Similarly his work in the field of *Professional Training* will be timed to enable him to design structurally in the various materials he is studying. He will study the construction types and methods appropriate to the materials singly and in combination. At the same time he will be required to develop simple structural forms with these materials, and then, as a result of the knowledge so gained, he will be required to detail original structural forms in the various materials.

This study of materials and construction will be carried beyond the older building materials and methods into the investigation of the manufactured and synthetic materials available today. The student will analyze the newer materials and make experiments to determine their proper uses, their proper combination in construction, their aesthetic possibilities and architectural forms appropriate to them.

This stage of the student's work is designed to give him a thorough knowledge of the means with which he must later build, a feeling for materials and construction and to teach him how architectural forms are developed from the necessities and possibilities inherent in materials and construction.

In the second major stage of the student's education, entitled *Purposes* on the program, the student will study the various purposes for which buildings are required in modern society. He will make a systematic study of the various functions of different kinds of buildings and seek reasonable solutions for their requirements from a technical, social and humanitarian standpoint. The construction, purpose, and arrangement of furniture and furnishings in their relation to the buildings and their occupants will also be studied.

After studying the requirements of various types of buildings and their solution, the student will progress to the study of ordering these types into groups and into unified communities — in other words: city planning. City planning will be studied from the point of view that the various parts of a community must be so related that the whole functions as a healthy organism. The student will also study the reorganization of existing cities to make them function as an organic unity. The possibilities of Regional planning will also be sketched.

Naturally the student's general theoretical education and professional training will be running along parallel to these studies and will be far enough advanced at each point so that he fully understands the technical, social and cultural aspects of each problem.

At the beginning of his study of the purposes of buildings, he will have begun the study of the nature of man; what he is, how he lives, how he works, what his needs are in both the material and spiritual sphere. He must also have an understanding of the nature of society; how man has organized himself into groups, apportioned and specialized his work to lighten it and allow him more leisure to pursue his spiritual aims and evolve a communal culture. This sociological study will also investigate former civilizations, their economic basis, their social forms, and the cultures which they produce.

The student will also study the history and nature of Technics — so that he may comprehend the compelling and supporting forces of modern society. He will learn the methods and principles of Technics and their implications in his own creative sphere. He will realize the new solutions of the problems of space, form and harmony made possible and demanded by the development of modern Technics.

The relationship between culture and technics will also be studied so that the student will be able to appreciate his part in developing a new culture so that finally our technical civilization may have a unified and integrated culture of its own.

Likewise the student's professional training will have advanced far enough at each point for him to solve the professional and technical factors of the problems that are being analyzed.

The third and last stage of the student's education has been entitled *Planning and Creating*.

When the student has advanced this far he will have mastered the technique of his profession; he will understand specific purposes and problems for which society requires his knowledge, and he will have acquired a general background which should have given him a thorough comprehension of modern life and have imbued him with a sense of professional and social obligation. He must now learn to use his knowledge of the means, and the purposes to produce architecture which is creative and living. This final and most important phase of his education is intended to enable him to do so.

During this phase of his education, all the facilities of the school will be directed towards training him in the fundamentals of creative design based upon the principles of organic order, so that he will attack his architectural problems with an essential philosophy whose guidance will enable him to create true architecture.